To Rag

All the very
best to you and
the gang at
Shutterfly.

Jim Martellu

The Power to Innovate

Rewiring the Minds of
Individuals and Organizations

by

James K. Marstiller, Jr. and
Jennifer Joerding Fickeler, Ph.D.

authorHOUSE™

1663 LIBERTY DRIVE, SUITE 200
BLOOMINGTON, INDIANA 47403
(800) 839-8640
WWW.AUTHORHOUSE.COM

First published by AuthorHouse 04/13/05

ISBN: 1-4208-3510-6 (dj)

Library of Congress Control Number: 2005901287

Printed in the United States of America
Bloomington, Indiana

This book is printed on acid-free paper.

Acknowledgments

This book is a product of research, thinking, combined experience, and most importantly, passion for the pursuit of innovation. This labor of love could not have been possible without the assistance, guidance, and support of several key individuals.

We would like to first thank our intellectual property attorney, Thomas Nutter, who was the first person to have confidence in our proposed idea of writing a book and consulting in the area of innovation. Tom was the first to say "If this thing goes public, let me be the first to buy stock in your company." His guidance and unending enthusiasm for our work was instrumental in our success.

Several key individuals who we identified as content experts in the area of innovation were integral to our success: Steve Crimmins, Randy Rose, James White, Jim Holbrook, John McGinty, Dr. Tom Kramer, Phil Harkins, Wilton Connor, and John Vella. We thank each one of these book reviewers for assisting us in the development and formation of our ideas. Each one has exemplified the true essence of innovation and success.

We are also greatly appreciative of the efforts of those individuals who helped us early on in the publishing process. Alice Feinstein provided invaluable editorial assistance and support. Our friend, Jim Hunter, provided timely feedback and support from one author to another. We are indebted to him for providing us with the encouragement to proceed as we translated our thoughts into book form. Later, the wonderful people at AuthorHouse provided us with the insight and guidance to make the publishing of this book a reality.

Last, but not least, we are deeply indebted to our respective families throughout this, sometimes, arduous process. We simply could not have made it to this point without their love, support, and encouragement.

For Lisa, Madeline, Robbie, and Sven, we thank you.

Contents

"If I would have asked people what they wanted they would have said a faster horse"
Henry Ford

A Preface in Four "mini-chapters"

Part 1: A Journey of an Entirely Different Sort – by James K. Marstiller, Jr.

Although I have been accused of being innovative consistently throughout my life and career, I never really thought of myself as being particularly "creative" (and I'm certain that I never thought much about the difference between innovation and creativity either). To me, being creative seemed to have a certain stigma to which I couldn't relate and didn't particularly want to. I thought of creative people as perhaps having green hair, multiple piercings, tattoos, being into the arts, putting things into their bodies that I would never dream of and/or working at Ad Agencies. "Creatives" surely had degrees in anthropology, art, design, music or literature. Or maybe they had no education at all. These people were just geniuses somehow and the rest of us were not.

Take Bob Dylan for example. Bob Dylan had no college education other than one ill-fated semester at the University of Minnesota - and Dylan is:

1) A certified creative genius.
2) One of the most influential poets and musicians of the 20th century and

3) A genuine legend in his own time. The Beatles paid attention to what Bob Dylan was doing!

One of my favorite Dylan stories was about his brief college education. While at the University of Minnesota, Dylan, (a.k.a. Bobby Zimmerman – his real name), took a course in communication. Legend has it that he called his teacher every morning and reported in. "Hello, this is Bobby Zimmerman, and I won't be coming to your class today". He reasoned that he communicated better than anyone in his class and that his teacher would never forget his name. Now I liked that – this guy had an attitude for sure! But basically I was nothing like Bob Dylan other than the fact that I couldn't sing. I'm much more conservative- in a Midwestern kind of way.

No, I was not a genius. I was a B/B+ student (but I took some solace in the fact that the average millionaire in America was a B student as well). My education is in science and business, not what I thought of as the domain of true creative types. But in spite of this background, I had this repeated history of being associated with innovation.

This followed me from assignment to assignment throughout my entire career. This history began in the 1st year of my career, when I was in Product R&D. At that time, I was awarded a "Special award for Innovation" and received a $1000 cash award. I didn't really think at the time that it was anything particularly creative. No, I had just applied something I had learned in microbiology while in graduate school that no one had quite thought of yet. The idea did have solid commercial application though and gave our company a distinct edge vs. our competition (and getting some cash was certainly O.K. with me as well).

This history of being associated with innovation, including patents, continued to follow me consistently throughout my career. A few examples of innovation where I was directly involved include the following:

- The creation of a new process which made pet foods significantly more palatable
- The creation of our company's "electronic library"

- The creation of our company's first CD ROM for external communication purposes
- The creation of a revolutionary approach to Solution Selling – an Industry first
- Several patented approaches for making Veterinary Hospitals more productive – Industry firsts.

One particular innovation though stands apart from the others. The one for which I was awarded the Innovator of the Year Award in 2000 (note: I was also fortunate enough to have won this award in 2001).

At that time, I was serving as a Vice President and Managing Director in a Sales capacity within Nestlé, one of the largest companies in the world. The innovation award was for the creation of an industry-leading "Learning Center". This Learning Center featured our best practices as a company and also leveraged our vendor relationships to maximum advantage. Not only did it help the organization accelerate learning, it repeatedly gave our sales force an enormous competitive advantage. This facility, which cost a little over $1 million to construct, paid for itself within the first few months of opening in the spring of 2000. Since that time it has generated countless millions in incremental business, has greatly strengthened customer relationships, has accelerated the company's ability to learn and be trained, and has saved millions in other efficiencies (including mistake avoidance). The Learning Center has been featured in the annual report and the accolades have been recorded from thousands of visitors from all over the world.

This was pretty heady stuff. However, I still considered my strengths to be leadership, business acumen, and management skills – not "soft stuff" like innovation. Where I worked, for example, we had a sophisticated process to measure your leadership ability. Long story short, I was consistently ranked in the top 10% of all the leaders in our Division. I could relate to that, and was proud of "my score". I mean, we had some hard data here.

When it came to innovation though, that was a different story. I thought almost anybody could do what I did if they just worked hard enough and kept their focus. Then I got a real surprise. Of all places, it came in the form of a test. On a whim, I took this test that was supposed to measure several aspects of your personality – you know, those "soft skills" that are traditionally not measurable. There were 12 categories in which I was thoroughly tested. One of the categories was labeled "creativity". Consistent with my history of test-taking, I was average on most scores, a little higher on some, and a little lower on others - except this one area that was labeled "creativity". In this area, I scored 32 out of a possible 33. This was so much higher than my other 11 categories. According to the historical database, this score was "off the charts". I was genuinely surprised.

It was now time to face the music. <u>Like it or not, without green or purple hair, and not being a genius, I must be some sort of "Creative" or Innovator.</u> How could this be? What was going on here? I mean, I really had to think about this.

Actually, the thinking was tucked away for about six months. Tucked away for a while and then brought out again almost involuntarily. Brought out actually while driving through the middle of Iowa in what seemed liked an endless ocean of corn. I was on my way to a self-prescribed mid-life adventure, an adventure that was to culminate in a solo wilderness journey in Canada, but more on that later.

I had been driving by myself about five hours from my home in St. Louis by now and was in the middle of Iowa. I had gone through all my favorite classic rock CDs – Led Zeppelin, Beatles, Eric Clapton, Crosby Stills, Nash and Young and of course Bob Dylan. I was getting bored and sore and I was out of cell phone range. I thought of Mark Twain's famous quote, "<u>Thinking</u> is the hardest work that man can do, and that is why so little of it is ever done". Feeling a bit guilty at this point for not being "productive" all day, even though I was on vacation, I started to do some thinking. I had all day and there was literally nothing else to do. There weren't even any cows to look at. I began thinking about innovation again. I began thinking hard. What was it that I was doing that kept leading to these results?

I took a page out of Stephen Covey's Masterpiece, <u>The 7 Habits of Highly Effective People</u> and decided to begin with the end in mind. So

I thought long and hard about the example of the "Learning Center". I thought about it in retrospect.

- If the Learning Center, for example, was the end result worthy of the company's highest innovation award, what were the drivers that allowed it to happen?
- Were they the same variables that had allowed me to develop other creative solutions?
- Did I notice the same parameters at work in other examples of applied innovation in my industry?
- How about throughout history – those great innovations that led to totally new businesses or those which saved lives?
- What were the patterns in human behavior?
- Were the same characteristics evident in other people that I personally knew who had been highly successful (with innovation being a key deliverable)?

I kept thinking about it and asking myself "why?" This was done until there was no more explanation – the answers had become self-evident. I asked myself so many questions for so many hours that my head hurt. This is something I think we rarely do.

The Genesis of Innovative Aptitude

I thought about the influence of my upbringing. Could that have something to do with it? Perhaps my parents had something to do with all this. I began to think more and more about my father and his influence, particularly on my attitude.

My father was a brilliant man and a gentleman. He was quite literally, a rocket scientist. With a Masters in Mathematics from MIT and a degree in Aerospace Engineering, my father was a key contributor to our nation's defense and space programs. But I wasn't like him. I didn't have his book smarts in math or his disposition. He could be painfully slow and engineer-like. I was much more entrepreneurial by nature (maybe that's a nice way of saying impatient). Even though our natures and our skills were different, we were very close personally. His influence had a profound effect on me, and the way I see things. He was the best man in my wedding.

By the time I had driven through Iowa and reached the Minnesota border, I had discerned two major influences that my father had in my life. They were self-evident and unmistakable. They explain how I see things – or literally - how I am "hardwired".

1. As a child, I was literally never allowed to say the words "I can't". My father told us over and over again that 'I can't', never did anything". Dad was never overly authoritarian or threatening in any way. However, this was drummed into me as a fact of life, a truism, just like the sun coming up in the morning. It was a fact of nature and I accepted it into my soul. This had a profound impact on me. The net effect was that, for me, the question was never, if something could be done, it was only how. This influenced how I saw everything in life and everyone. To me, people that would question whether or not something could be done, or worse yet, could articulate, why it couldn't be done, just plain didn't "get it". They were either lazy or negative in my mind. They were fundamentally addressing the wrong question. As a result, I wasn't particularly interested in someone's opinion on why something couldn't be done.

    The famous quote from Henry Ford rang true to me. As background here, Ford was furious at his board members who had brought him "the experts" who had articulated why his vision of the assembly line wouldn't work. Ford thundered at them, "Damn it! Don't bring me the world's experts to tell me why the thing can't do done, bring me the young men who will do it!" For Henry Ford, the question was never <u>if</u>, it was only <u>how</u>. He already knew the answer. He already <u>knew</u> that it could be done. He already knew the end result. That made sense to me too. If you were not on board with Henry, you were in the way. To quote another auto industry icon, Lee Iacocca, "Either lead, follow, or get out of the way!"

2. As a child, Dad would say to me, "Son, either you do, or you don't". The upshot here was there are no excuses. It's painfully simple, either you do or you don't. There are no excuses and

you are personally responsible for your actions. Again, this was internalized as an indisputable fact of nature.

"Do or do not, there is no try"

Yoda

I vividly remember an application of this principle while I was in high school. Here was the deal: if I was to be eligible for the car keys for the weekend, the grass had to be cut by sundown Friday. On one particular Friday, I was late coming home. Track practice lasted longer than I had anticipated and I stopped by a friend's house on the way home. Then it started to rain and of course the grass became too wet to cut. What happened? I didn't even have to bother to ask for the keys. The grass wasn't cut and I wasn't eligible for the car. Period. No excuses and I was the one who was responsible. I could have:

- Checked the weather forecast and gotten home earlier to cut the grass or
- I could have cut the grass earlier in the week.

But I knew it was my fault and that I was responsible. To blame anyone or anything for my mistake was just unacceptable. It was up to me.

There's good news and bad news in this fundamental truth. There is a positive side of course, and that is if you want to accomplish something you can. It's all up to you and excuses are not relevant. Like Nike – Just do it.

The foundation of my personal hardwiring is a combination of these two truths – Never think in terms of 1) "I can't" or "it can't be done" and 2) no excuses.

While these may explain an attitudinal makeup, they do not identify the <u>specific attributes of human behavior</u> that lead to innovation. In order to flesh those out, I would need to spend a lot more time thinking. Fortunately my circumstances would allow me to do this. I still had another day's drive to my Canadian destination, eight days alone in the wilderness, and the 1000-mile drive home.

I had been doing a lot of thinking, and true to Mark Twain's quote, I was worn out. However, I felt that I was beginning to make some sense out of what made me tick on the innovation front. I was feeling a sense of satisfaction as I closed in on my destination in Duluth. I also knew I had a long way to go – both figuratively and literally. It was now time to put my favorite CDs back in and head north - to Canada to my big adventure and forget about the variables of innovation for awhile. The adventure of a lifetime awaited me.

Part 2: Finding the Way - A Time Alone in the Wilderness

No attempt will be made in this book to detail my eight-day, 75-mile solo trek, through the wilderness. Here is the top line though. The Quetico Provincial Wilderness area in Ontario is remote and pristine. It is a vast area covering approximately 5,000 square kilometers, roughly the same size as Yellowstone, yet much more isolated. There are literally no roads of any kind. There is no hunting, trapping or logging. There are thousands of lakes, many of which are interconnected and they are drinking-water pure. The only viable mode of transportation is by canoe. No motors of any kind are allowed. Paddle power only. Between lakes, you carry your gear, including your canoe.

The area is rich in history. Indian tribes have inhabited this area for thousands of years. There are pictographs, made from bear grease and iron ore, still evident on the rock cliffs. The small trails, or portages, between the lakes are the same ones that the native Indian tribes used many years ago. These are also the same lakes and trails that the fur trade used to get their product back to Rainy Lake and Fort Francis, Ontario (a.k.a. "civilization"). The French Fur trade flourished here during the 18th and early 19th centuries. It is easy to imagine the French Voyageurs in their large birch bark canoes carrying their precious cargo of 90-pound fur-bundles and singing in cadence to their paddle strokes.

The Quetico Provincial wilderness area has abundant wildlife. It has innumerable beaver, moose, coyotes, fox, lynx, deer, black bears, ducks of every description, bald eagles and ospreys and more. You really haven't heard the call of the wild until you hear the eerie and haunting call of the Northern Loon at night. If you are really lucky, you may hear the wolves.

If well prepared, a trip through Quetico can be fantastic. The fishing can be spectacular – Small mouth bass, Northern Pike, Walleye and Lake Trout. The wilderness beauty and camaraderie of close friends is priceless. The sense of satisfaction that comes from a hard day's physical labor is its own reward. Being away from the everyday pressures of life, including our technological conveniences is also a blessing.

If you are not well prepared, or have bad luck, a trip through Quetico can be a nightmare. The wilderness is unforgiving. The wilderness is not a game. There are no second chances if something goes wrong. If someone is hurt, help is almost always days away. It is an area of violent weather shifts. Some of North America's most violent storms are brewed in this area just north of the Great Lakes. In July 2000, a storm packing 100+ mile wind knocked down countless trees over thousands of acres. It can snow in July. The temperature can shift 40 degrees within hours. A capsizing can cause lethal hypothermia. There are bears, wolves, and moose in Quetico. You can easily get turned around and lost. The lakes and their islands can look eerily alike. Landmarks can be indistinguishable. The portages, or trails between lakes, are not marked, and sometimes cannot be found. The maps are not always accurate.

I have been to the Canadian Wilderness many times, but always with a group of other experienced guys. This was my first time alone. If you are alone, all these variables and threats intensify.

Here is a summation of my trip:
- It was different than I thought it would be. Much different alone than with a group.
- The every day responsibilities of cooking, camping, cleaning, canoeing, portaging and navigating are all-consuming.
- This journey represented the most physically grueling work I've ever done (and I've done a lot!)
- I loved it and was exhausted at the same time.
- My outfitter forgot to supply me a life jacket. Being a purist, I had no satellite phone either.

- Some of my perspectives will be changed forever and that's good.
- The survival or animal part of your being begins to emerge. Your hearing becomes amazingly acute after the third day.
- You become very cognizant of your environment and it's relation to your well being.
- You pay attention to the wind and weather in ways you wouldn't think possible.
- I saw amazing things, including the survival of the fittest – as follows:
  - A beautiful bald eagle snatching a fish off the surface of the lake without missing a wing beat.
  - A huge Northern Pike (almost four feet long) literally attack the smallmouth bass that I was reeling in for "my dinner".
  - A dragon fly pluck a spider right out of its own web and eat it on the spot – in mid-air!
  - Pine trees that seemed to be growing right out of the sides of the granite cliffs – clinging to life.
- I also saw the Northern lights, or Aurora Borealis, nature's indescribable, and fantastic, laser-show in the sky.
- It was obvious that the wilderness doesn't care about money, status, business, accomplishments, cars, titles or politics. There is only one task and that is to survive.
- Over 60 pages were recorded in a journal that my wife encouraged me to bring "in case I felt like writing". I thought about my family, friends, and what's really important.
- I sustained a leg injury that later required surgery.
- I almost capsized on a large lake taking on waves that I shouldn't have – a near-death survival experience.
- Your mind becomes cleansed of the daily noise of life and you gain new insights and perspectives that are deep and good.
- I got in touch with feelings including loneliness, fear, and faith.
- And yes, I will do it again.

Part 3: Together in Some Things -
Alone in Self-Discovery

The important lessons that I learned had to do with loneliness, fear, and faith.

Loneliness is painful. I remember my brother John telling me before I left for this trip "I could never do what you are doing, I'd get too lonely". I also remember my foolish response, "John, I don't even know what loneliness is". In the corporate world you are overwhelmed by people and communication devices – pagers, PDAs, cell phones, fax machines, etc. When you get home from work, the kids mob you. The wife needs some time too! There are constant social responsibilities. But lonely? No way, I won't feel that. Let me tell you, after about five days of talking to NOBODY – not saying a word, you begin to understand lonely. I understand why people talk to themselves. I began to relate in some small way why Tom Hanks invented "Wilson" in the movie Castaway.

Loneliness is a hurt in the gut. It's a longing that we humans need. I will never look at those who are potentially lonely again in the same light - older people, the new neighbors, or shut-ins. Maybe there might be a little something that I could do to ease their pain.

Fear isn't much fun either. Our daily lives are largely devoid of real fear. Our neighborhoods are relatively safe, we have police and fire protection, we have our burglar alarms, and our cars have air bags. We also have grocery stores full of food. We have the best medical treatment in the world. If all else fails we even have "insurance". It's been a long time since us humans, as a species, have had to feel real fear – primal fear. The fear associated with your ship going down on the high seas or the fear of being devoured by a wild beast.

While it does get pretty dark at night in Quetico, I had little to fear from wild beasts. Although one night I did think that a bear was in my camp. It turned out to be a porcupine! This gets the blood pumping nonetheless I can assure you! I did however, tie my food in the trees as a precaution - call this "practical insurance".

No, my primal fear experience occurred in my canoe. I pushed the envelope a little too far one day and put myself in a very dangerous and life- threatening, situation.

A common strategy in the North Country is to get up early and paddle before the wind picks up. It almost always does in the summer as the heat of the day increases. You can pretty much count on this happening. A common strategy is to paddle in the morning, then keep your eyes open during the middle of the day for wind and waves, and then paddle again in the evening after the waves have died down. You always have your eyes on the sky to monitor the weather and the clouds – and the waves. Canoes are made incredibly light these days. My craft was a 16' model made of Kevlar and, unloaded, weighed only 34 pounds! It was so thin-skinned that the light clearly shone through it. It is made lightweight for easy carrying and paddling. It is not made to withstand high seas. By now, you can pretty much guess what I got myself into, over a mile from shore, with no life jacket, and many, many miles from other people.

I had finished lunch by about 1:00 P.M., it was getting warmer and the wind was picking up. Right on schedule. White caps were beginning to appear on the lake. I could even see my island destination for the day, only about four miles down the lake. At this point there was a fundamental decision to make. Should I stay put and make camp here, or press forward to my original destination?

Part 4: Ego Management: A Must for Survival and a Must for Innovation

I began to reason, "I can make it now! Yes, it's starting to get rough, but the waves don't look all that bad. And if I can just sprint to that long peninsula – maybe 30 minutes of hard paddling - I'll find shelter from the waves. Hey I can sprint for 30 minutes!!" I had talked myself into a very bad idea. Ego over reason almost cost me dearly.

I started to go - paddling hard. I was tired and didn't quite have the strength I had the previous day. No Problem, "suck it up" I could hear my old track coach say. Ten minutes out and it was pretty obvious that those white caps were quite a bit higher than they had looked from shore. Now this canoe, fully loaded, was no more than a foot higher than the waterline. The waves were now running at about three feet high as the lake widened. Uncomfortable for sure, but still doable as long as the canoe is moving ahead at a fast pace (if the canoe is not moving quickly enough in windy weather, you *lose your ability to steer*). I raced on, paddling harder and harder, using all my concentration, and looking straight ahead.

The wind picked up even more as I entered the widest part of the lake, where the wind blew unobstructed for almost three miles. The gusts had now grown to over 20 knots. A few waves now began to break over the top of my canoe. I'll never forget what I saw as I glanced into the wind to my right – white capped waves between four and five feet tall bearing down on me!! I felt a real rush of fear, but not panic. It's funny how your mind works in these situations. For me, I felt intense concentration and a feeling of slow-motion or time-compression. I knew I couldn't fail. Failure was not an option here. I couldn't capsize this boat. The consequences were too high. If the canoe capsized, at best, I would survive with no gear of any kind, several days from another rescue. It was at this moment that I decided to turn the canoe 90 degrees and get that wind and those waves straight behind me. I would then sprint with everything I had left in me to a small island about a ½ mile away. If I could get behind it, I would be safe. The waves were now picking up the canoe and carrying it like a surfboard and threatening to swamp me from behind.

I made it. I got behind that island, pulled my canoe ashore and lashed it to a tree. I was utterly exhausted in every way. I listened to the wind howl and just looked out across the water I had crossed. I got out pictures of my kids and held them in my hands. I gave thanks to God and didn't leave that spot for several hours until the wind died down. Yes, I felt fear that day, but it wasn't all bad. It was just part of the process of understanding that you are just a very small part of something very big. I also came away with a renewed sense that everything would be O.K. and that I was being watched over.

It was also good in that I now have much more empathy for those that may be afraid. Whatever their circumstances might be.

The Long Drive Back

In retrospect, I really didn't think about the variables of innovation while I was in the wilderness. I was too busy being preoccupied with getting through each day. I am certain however that all the thoughts that I had on the long drive to Canada had been incubating. They were now waiting to come out of a mind that had been cleansed and rested through the wilderness experience. It was on that long drive back, again through the corn of Iowa, where the thinking about innovation began again in earnest.

Three things were fleshed out:

- The outline for The Power to Innovate including the "four pillars of innovation".
- A clear understanding of what Innovation is not.
- The realization that the advice of experts in the science of Human Behavior would be absolutely invaluable (Dr. Jennifer Fickeler became that expert).

In general, the Four Pillars were derived using the same "begin with the end in mind" methodology that was used before, and of course, this resulted in more questions.

- What were the common human behaviors that led to a particular innovation, not only in my own experiences, but also in the meaningful innovations throughout history?
- What were those common behaviors or pillars?
- Once identified, how could they be translated to a meaningful framework?
- How could these pillars be measured in individuals and groups?
- What did the current scientific literature reveal about the four pillars of innovation?
- How could this learning be applied to individuals and groups?
- How can a culture of innovation be created?

The answers to these questions, and more, are what this book is all about.

Introduction

THE POWER TO INNOVATE
Rewiring the Minds of Individuals and Organizations

Writing this book was a labor of love fueled by a passion for the subject.

THE POWER TO INNOVATE fills a void that exists among the available books on innovation. This book bypasses current fads and focuses on the application and measurement of innovation for organizational and personal change.

Until now, no one had written a book that explains in plain English, *why* innovation occurs, and then how it can be delivered. Only through the combined experience of a global business executive, who had successfully delivered innovation, <u>*and*</u> the skill of a research and training professional, could this be accomplished and the "pillars of innovation" identified.

It was also discovered that breakthrough innovation is not random. It's predictable. The key is `to focus on what *causes* innovation to happen and then to nurture a culture that *allows* it to happen. For this to occur, the minds of individuals and organizations have to be rewired. There really is no other way. There are no short cuts.

The result is a breakthrough book that puts the power to innovate in your hands. THE POWER TO INNOVATE goes beyond explaining how to drive innovation in an organization; it also shows how to live a more innovative personal life. No other book goes this extra, key, next step - and the 90-day prescription self-help guides show the way.

Of course innovation is a very hot topic these days. The word INNOVATION is in many mission statements, in every organization around the world - and for good reason. There is a real sense of urgency surrounding the need to innovate to stay out in front. Nothing is more important in today's hyper-competitive market. It is absolutely straightforward: Add value or die. Differentiate or die. Innovate or die.

Innovation is the *only* source of sustainable competitive advantage.

Innovation is POWER.

We strove to give you that power.

THE POWER TO INNOVATE exceeds expectations in many ways including the focus on providing clarity, flexibility, and applicability.

THE POWER TO INNOVATE is clearly illustrated through the four "pillars" of innovation.
- Perseverance
- Knowledge
- Risk
- Passion

Each pillar is brought to life through real-world examples, the author's experiences and the latest research. The end result is a reading experience that is not only fact-based, but also entertaining and enjoyable. The truths revealed by example, logic and research quickly become self-evident. For example, it will be easily understood that if one of the pillars is not present, innovation *cannot* occur.

THE POWER TO INNOVATE also delivers great flexibility. The truths contained within are relevant to a very wide audience. The book makes sense for anyone responsible for nurturing and delivering innovation whether it is for huge corporate giants or entrepreneurs. It rings true not only for business and organizational leaders but also for teachers, engineers, accountants, nurses, and authors.

Lastly, the book is imminently practical. The material was designed for immediate application including:

- Building an innovative organization through a logical process.
- Practical advice on dealing with the barriers to innovation from Corporate Antibodies to Psychic Vampires.
- Delivering innovation through others.
- Demystifying the latest research into practical application.
- Understanding what innovation is, and is not, and how it differs from creativity.
- Creating a culture of innovation through rewiring the minds of those responsible for delivering it.

In short, THE POWER TO INNOVATE converts the know-how into the show-how.

Enjoy this book, use it, and take action!

Chapter One –
Barriers to Innovation

"Corporate Antibodies exist in every organization. They are comprised of those individuals who see it as their responsibility, and even their duty, to maintain the status quo at all costs - to stamp out and repudiate all new thoughts, ideas and inputs as they are perceived as a threat to their world"
                                            Randy Rose

"There are two ways to misrepresent the truth: lie or use statistics"
                                            Mark Twain

"Which is it with you son - ignorance or apathy? Dad, I don't know and I don't care"
                                            Old Joke

"Keep an eye out for Psychic Vampires and avoid them like the plague"
                                            Jack Reilley

"Ladies and gentlemen step right up and see the giant lizard!!
27 feet from the tip of his nose to the tip of his tail - and 27' feet
from the tip of his tail to the tip of his nose – totaling 54 feet in
all! Yes, come see the giant lizard!"

A Circus Barker – 1910

The Big One

Why is breakthrough innovation so rare? The answer is because there are so many things that have to go right for it to occur.

Achieving breakthrough innovation is like catching a trophy fish. That fish that is so special that it is cherished above all others. The one that is known among friends, relatives, and co-workers simply as "the fish". If there is a fire in your house, you tell the fireman "save the photos of me and the fish!" (And grab the wedding pictures too while you are in there). This fish is so special because you've fished your whole life and only caught one this big. This one is a standard deviation bigger than all the others. On that special day, everything went right. This fish - this trophy – is so rare because there were so many things that could have gone wrong. Here is a partial list.

- The line must be the correct strength (too light and the fish will break it off - too heavy and the fish will see it and not bite)
- The rod must be stout enough (but not too stout)
- The reel must be in perfect working order (and the all-important "drag" needs to be set just right – that sweet spot between too tight and not tight enough).
- The line must be in perfect condition. A microscopic nick in the line will cause it to break under the strain of the big one.
- All the knots must hold.
- The big one cannot get snagged or cut the line on some underwater obstacle (not the least of which is its teeth)
- The hooks must be sharp enough to sink in and strong enough to hold.

Again, it's a partial list, and we haven't even talked about the skill of the angler and his (or her) knowledge of fish and their environment.

Yes, breakthrough innovation is something like that. Does this mean that breakthrough innovation only happens once in an individual or organization's lifetime? Absolutely not. Delivering innovation is not a random occurrence. Everyone knows that some consistently do it better than others. There are reasons for this. Specific reasons.

It is true that 20% of the fishermen catch 80% of the fish. It is also true that 2% of the fishermen catch 98% of the *trophy* fish. Why? They have isolated the variables down to a predictable few and then stacked all the odds in their favor through their approach. For them the process is not left to random chance.

Similarly, this book is not about making the impossible happen through the random intersection of ideas. This book is about moving from the random to the predictable. The key is to rewire minds through an understanding of why innovation occurs and then nurturing a culture that allows it to happen. There really is no other way.

The truth is, in today's environment, you *need* to be an innovator to survive. It's not optional anymore. So buckle up your seat belt and make sure the air bag is working. This is going to be a bumpy ride. This isn't going to be easy. Keep an eye out for obstacles. There are even some who would like to see you in the ditch. Just as there are barriers to catching trophy fish, there are obstacles to achieving breakthrough innovation.

Barriers to Innovation

There are many barriers to innovation ranging from attitudinal, to cultural, and to practical and everything in between. There is no end to the lengths that individuals, and groups, will go to squelch new thinking and cling doggedly to the past. It's human nature!

As someone who is associated with delivering innovation, you will want to be prepared on how to identify these barriers and address them when they arise.

In general, the barriers to innovation are simply the opposite of the four pillars upon which this book is based.

The Opposite of PASSION = Passionless: apathetic, indifferent and low energy

The Opposite of PERSEVERANCE = The Quitter: he who gives up or does not pursue.

The Opposite of KNOWLEDGE = Ignorant: lacking understanding, myopic and unconnected.

The Opposite of RISK = Visionless: conservative, backward looking and uncourageous

It's obvious that those who are passionless quitters, and who lack knowledge and vision, are not the types to be placed in charge of delivering innovation. It is guaranteed that the person who lacks passion and knowledge, who won't take a risk, and who is unwilling to persevere, will <u>never</u> invent anything of commercial value.

My experience has taught me that there are barriers to innovation which range from the subtle to the sublime. Let's examine a few.

From Corporate Antibodies to Psychic Vampires

Perhaps the largest barrier to innovation is attitudinal.

As such, Corporate Antibodies are those who feel it is *their duty* to squelch all new thinking, at all costs, "for the good of the company". If fresh ideas or concepts are injected into the organization's body, *then* it is the Corporate Antibody's job to kill them.

Corporate Antibodies exist in every organization: corporations large and small, even non-profits including churches and the local Boy Scout troop. Generally these are not bad people. We all could name a few who qualify.

Often what's going on is that these people are easily threatened when the status quo is questioned in some way. As a reaction to this perceived threat, they often strike back in one of two ways.

- Question the innovator's work
- Question the innovator's motives

The Tyranny of Data

Often the questioning of the innovator's work will have some basis in "data". Of course as human beings, we put great faith in data – those studies, numbers, or statistics that can be used to quantify things. You cannot run a business without data and you cannot innovate without it either. However, when taken to the extreme, a certain critical balance can be lost. Caution has to be taken that we don't only bow down to those things that are quantifiable (like financial statements). The cart can be put before the horse; forgetting that it is people who are driving the numbers and not the other way around. In other cases we simply put "blinders on the horse" and use data to justify our own point of view so we don't have to consider the views of others.

Data can be very misleading. Perhaps Mark Twain said it best: *"There are two ways to misrepresent the truth: lie and use statistics".*

The implication is obvious; data can be manipulated to say just about anything we want it to say. To use data to protect our currently held beliefs is a natural defense mechanism and is likely linked to our personal sense of security.

The most common way that data can be used as a barrier to new thought is what I call the "rear view mirror syndrome". Much data is gathered in arrears. In other words it represents events that have happened in the past. This is all fine, EXCEPT, what the innovator is working on is the future. Quite simply, much – if not all, of what has happened in the past is IRRELEVANT to the future that the innovator is visualizing. As a result, looking at data, which represents the events of the past, is like looking in the rear view mirror of a car and determining where to go next. That technique is O.K. as long as the road ahead of the car looks exactly like the road the car has been on. If that road twists to the left or right, or goes off-road or if there is a moose in the middle of the road – there will be a major problem!

I vividly recall years ago when I used data in that very way. I used data (erroneously!) to justify my own previously held position and the sanctity of the data itself. Here is what happened. I had just joined a new team that was focusing on warehouse clubs like Sam's and Costco.

We were putting together our annual business plans. I had come from the Marketing department where data was king. Marketing was proud of its reputation for being buttoned-up. There was a chart and exhibit for everything – each one chock full of data. But now I was working with sales guys and they had a very different mindset. They didn't seem to be as concerned with data as I was. When it came down to estimating the size of the club market, I thought it was pretty obvious what the ONLY approach should be. You simply looked at the data. The data, in this case, showed 20% growth for each of the past 5 years. It was obvious therefore that next year's growth would be 20%. Pretty simple I thought. To think otherwise would not be fact-based. Well the head salesperson, in charge of Club growth, had a different perspective, one not based on data. He said that the market wouldn't grow more than 5%. His source of data? He had talked to the CEO of Sam's Club who had shared that due to economic conditions, they (and likely Costco as well) would be greatly reducing the number of new stores built the following year.

My reaction, I'm embarrassed to say, was *SO* TYPICAL of data-centered people. My thinking went like this, "Typical sales guys, shooting from the hip……..no data, probably just 'sandbagging' his sales forecast so he can make his bonus". Well guess what, the market slowed to 5% growth that year exactly as the executive from Sam's had projected and my "data" was totally wrong! In retrospect, think how preposterous, how absolutely arrogant, my position was. I was in essence saying "I don't care if you had a personal conversation with the person who knows more about Clubs than anyone else in the world – the guy who actually runs them – I have data!"

Yikes, what an idiot I was. I'm comforted though in knowing that this is just the nature of data-focused people. I've learned and I've changed. It's called experience. No amount of data can replace experience and all that glitters is not gold. Again, I'm not bashing data; you can't run a business or organization without it. But like everything in life there needs to be a balance. That balance between data and common sense, vision and experience.

–It may be recalled that in 1978 the CEO of IBM stated that there was "absolutely no need for the average American household to have a computer". Kind of missed the boat on that one, I'd say. Here's the point: did any one company in the world have more data than IBM in 1978? Arguably not. A couple of people named Bill Gates and Steven Jobs had something more valuable. They had a vision – and a boatload of each of the four pillars: Perseverance, Knowledge, Risk and Passion.

Importantly, here's what you need to know when dealing with heavily data-focused people and departments (e.g. Engineering, Market Research, Accounting, or Finance)

Like me at the time, they <u>"listen for" data</u> – numbers, statistics, study results, etc. To them, your credibility is directly associated with the data you share. No data – no credibility. You can take them through your rationale, you can share the perspectives of industry experts who support your line of reasoning, and you can share testimonials from important people who have tested your idea. It will all be in vain! With these people, if they don't hear "the data", they assume you are basically BS'ing them.

This train of thought can often lead to a second nasty consequence – <u>it gets personal</u>.

- They assume you are BS'ing them, and therefore <u>you</u> can't be trusted.
- They assume that you must be working your own agenda.
- They are threatened by your vision of what might be happening next because they feel that's their turf!
- Their rearview mirror data doesn't jive with your vision. Never will.

Unfortunately, I have seen these circumstances unfold many different times. Here is what I recommend:

1. Don't get mad or make it personal. Always be pleasant and professional. Remember, you are dealing with people who are <u>not</u> visionaries. They are not like you. They are "measurers" or they are late adapters. They may even be "corporate weathervanes" who will only jump on board *after* they know

which way the political wind is blowing. Perhaps they have chosen their profession because their sense of personal security is linked to the certainty of things measured. Who knows?! If you get mad at them though for not visualizing what you clearly see, it won't help.

2. It is always wise to share whatever data is available. It might not be much, but learn to share. Take them through your process. These people typically love process, so convert your thoughts to a process. Call it a through z and use terms that they can relate to. Ask them how they would go about measuring what you are working on. Don't exclude them, involve them.

3. Gain their trust as individuals. Take them to lunch invite them to sporting events with you; tell them about what you are doing in your life. They will come to know you as a person and not a threat.

4. Keep your supervisor in the loop. Corporate Antibodies love to take their "grievances" concerning your work over your head to your boss. As a result, you will want him to be well informed about the facts and prepared to offer support.

5. Don't worry about it! Sometimes this can be really hard. You have so much passion for what you believe in and you have to work with these idiot skeptics! Change your attitude, seek your supervisor's support, and have faith.

Of course, Corporate Antibodies are not always just data-centered people. There are always people that for whatever reason just don't want to change. The whole idea of change seems threatening to them, as change doesn't always:

- Follow the tried and true
- Follow the rules
- Follow "how things are done around here" or
- Follow the process

Creating the future through innovation isn't about following anything of course. It's about leading. New leadership, even thought-leadership, may be threatening to those who see a particular area or discipline as their turf.

My advice would be to treat these people in the same way you would the data-junkies. When it comes to corporate antibodies, remember what Abraham Lincoln said, *"stay close to your friends, and even closer to your enemies"*. Don't adopt the mindset that these data-centered people are your enemies, but remember to stay close to them. Consider, that some of these people may never be your best friend (as your views of the world are so fundamentally different), but if you can move them from doubtful skeptic to "neutral", that just might be a wonderful victory.

Psychic Vampires

Another barrier to innovation can be the psychic vampire. You'll recall that a psychic vampire is someone who has a penchant for sucking the very joy out of life itself. This is the person who, on the beautiful 75-degree day, comments, "I heard it's supposed to rain this weekend". These people are energy-takers. They are negative. They can conjure up the negative in everything. We all know people like this. My advice with these people is simple – avoid them at all costs. They can do your psyche and your career no good. It is also guaranteed that these people do not impress management.

There is a second type of psychic vampire to be aware of because you might just have to work with one. This type can be in a position of importance but they are only experienced or proficient in one field. They sometimes have been around awhile and have interesting personality quirks. These people can honestly think they are doing their job by imaging all the reasons why something can't work. Maybe you know someone like this. Some of these people, engineers in particular, can actually be trained to think this way. This is the way they think and speak. They stay up at night (as vampires do of course) trying to think what could possibly go wrong. That's all they want to talk about.

There are other people that have this trait who of course are just jerks or losers. I used to work with someone in R&D who was like this. He was a PhD who we gave the nickname "Dr No". He could come up with a reason why everything couldn't work, or wouldn't pass the government testing, or something. There was always something.

He was exasperating to work with and he seemed to delight with his power to shut things down. These types of people don't give you the impression that they are willing to work with the group to find a way as much as they are throwing out stumbling blocks.

This type of psychic vampire drives innovators and sales people crazy. My experience has taught me that innovators and sales people have one interesting character trait in common. That is that they tend to be eternally optimistic. I think this is because they both have to deal with a lot of failure and rejection. The sales guy must believe that he is going to close the big one after being rejected five times previously. Similarly, the innovator must believe that next time his contraption will work, or management will see the light, or something. If these professions didn't have this attitude, they would never make it. They couldn't persevere and ultimately succeed without this eternal optimism.

If you let them, these people will drain you. Don't let them. I have found that they can rarely help you, but can hurt you and your cause. On rare occasions I have found that it might help if you have a frank conversation with them about how they are perceived by the team. In most cases it makes no difference whatsoever. If all else fails, keep in mind this comforting fact, if you have noticed this intensely irritating trait in someone, a lot of your peers have too.

Bottom line; keep an eye open for Corporate Antibodies, Psychic Vampires and related hobgoblins.

Creative Voodoo

Another barrier to innovation is the very people who make a living from it.

As in fields like physical fitness or nutrition, there can be a lot of voodoo operators among the real doctors. There seems to be an aura of magic or mysticism surrounding innovation that really need not be there. I can see though why there is though. Self-proclaimed creative gurus have perpetuated much of this thinking. Maybe you are familiar with some of them, —or you have attended a "creative workshop" or two. Unfortunately, some of this work falls into one of two closely related categories.

- Snake oil
- Frisbees and Slinkys

The terminology Snake oil is derived from the proverbial snake oil salesman. This refers, of course to the traveling salesman who peddles magical elixirs who promises to cure all ills from rheumatism to lumbago. Sadly, the snake oil salesman is alive and well. Millions of people are bilked out of countless dollars annually on schemes ranging from "get rich quick" to "stay young" to "cure arthritis". While there is frequently some thread of truth involved in what is being hawked, the primary motivation for the true snake oil salesman is to get rich, not help mankind. At best he is selling hope and at worst there is deliberate deceit.

What is more frequently found in the pursuit of innovation or creativity is what I call "Frisbees and Slinkys". The Frisbees and Slinkys approach involves attempts to generate creative thinking via a set of very unusual approaches, exercises, and venues. These approaches are often facilitated by a self-proclaimed, or industry-proclaimed, guru. These gurus can also sometimes come across as a screwball in terms of appearance, speech or mannerisms. If you didn't know upfront that these folks were "creativity experts" you might think they were a little flaky. That should send a warning signal to you, as you are not looking to create art for its own sake; you are looking to commercialize innovation. Anything less than a fully professional approach, someone that takes your business as seriously as you do, should be questioned.

The Frisbees and Slinkys approaches are limitless but the themes are all pretty similar. If you have ever found yourself in one of these situations, it's possible that you were at a Frisbees and Slinkys venue.

- Creative retreats where participants were required to do wild and wacky things including team building games and competitions where you felt foolish.
- Brainstorming sessions where toys and props were used

- Exercises that required you to build something out of blocks, bark like a dog (or squawk like a chicken), or pretend you were a famous person – or otherwise act like an idiot.
- You were asked to take a nap, or meditate, to get in touch with your deeper thoughts
- Your facilitators were kind of weird. If you were in sales you wouldn't let these people get anywhere near your customers.
- It was the whispered consensus of the group that this was a boondoggle.

It is not suggested that these venues add nothing of value. After all, if you can get away from the office for a day or two, and eat and drink on somebody else's nickel, AND if management endorses it, well then who is going to complain? What is suggested is that very little of LASTING VALUE is gained. No. What is more likely to develop is a scenario somewhat akin to the emperor's new clothes. It can go something like this:

Step 1: Management recognizes that there isn't much innovation going on (e.g. in new products, ad campaigns, sales approaches) and they need to do something – anything. They need to at least point out to their bosses that *they* are doing something – "…… that's right, we have a creativity seminar scheduled in June to boost our performance in this area………."

Step 2: The troops are advised that certain people will be attending a creativity seminar on a certain date, at a nice place and that "an expert" will be facilitating the whole thing. It will actually be kind of fun they say.

Step 3: The troops think, "What the heck, sounds like fun. We get to go to a nice place, we don't have to prepare anything, we are not held accountable for anything, and we eat and drink" What is there not to like?

Step 4: The event unfolds, the wild and wacky facilitator does his or her thing, everybody has a good time, there is a team photo and everybody goes home.

Step 5: When management wants to know "How was the creativity seminar?" The response? It was great. We had a good time, did a lot of interesting exercises that really made us think and we gained some new perspectives. Management presses – "We'll was it worthwhile?" Oh, yes – I think there were some ideas that we can apply to what we do around here….. (What is not said is this, *"Are you nuts? We goofed off for 2 days and you paid for it!"*).

Like the emperor's new clothes, the seminar attendees may be reluctant to give an accurate accounting. Whether it's a two day seminar, a one day session where the facilitator is brought in, or just a luncheon brainstorming session, there is precious little of lasting value that comes out of these things. Often the greatest value is associated with having people from different departments conversing face to face.

Why is this the case though? Why is it that these approaches often miss the mark? Like many tough questions, the answer is multifaceted.

1. We live in a quick fix society. We want to send people to a seminar and be done with it. A friend of mine calls this the "sheep dip" approach.
2. Changing human behavior is very difficult and takes time. Think for a moment about a behavior that you wanted to change within yourself and how hard that was. Now reflect upon how difficult it is to change someone else's behavior.
3. Changing an entire organization's culture is even harder. Think for a moment about someone you may know who personally has changed the culture of an organization. It would be suggested that this person a) expended an enormous amount of energy and b) would tell you it was the hardest thing they ever did. Of course, the only way a culture changes is by the leadership and involvement of one person.

Why Brainstorming Sessions Rarely Work

A very common technique for attempting to generate new ideas is the brainstorming session.

Brainstorming sessions have:

- Good intentions
- Smart People
- Smiling Faces and
- Pizza

So what's the problem? What's not to like about this? Everything!

Brainstorming sessions often lack structure, a serious business objective, a process, accountability and leadership. Let's examine each of these in a bit more detail to uncover the pitfalls associated with these sessions and what a better approach might be.

Very often brainstorming sessions lack structure. Specifically, they often lack a written agenda, meeting prep work, and a specific objective. These things are germane to successful business meetings and should be with brainstorming sessions as well. When is the last time you attended a brainstorming session where these things were done?

Often the expectations surrounding a brainstorming session are low. After all, it's "only a brainstorming session" seems to be the norm. I'm all for fun, but there almost always seems to be a party atmosphere when it comes to these things. How can you expect to have real breakthrough ideas when people aren't mentally prepared to work hard? This is folly. There seems to be an attitude that follows these sessions which goes like this, "Are you going to Joe's brainstorming session today at noon (wink, wink) – he's bringing in pizza from Rizzotti's!!" Hey, if people aren't serious, what can be expected?

One last thing that seems to doom these sessions is that they lack leadership. Specifically, the facilitator doesn't properly prepare the meeting attendees or set the expectations high enough. All these things will hinder truly breakthrough thinking.

As you can tell, I'm not a big advocate of brainstorming sessions. I can guarantee you that the assembly line, the PC, the microwave oven, the cell phone and sliced bread were not the end result of these. The typical brainstorming session isn't going to generate your next big breakthrough.

The reason that brainstorming sessions are rarely productive is that to truly generate breakthrough ideas you will have to work harder than ever before! Brainstorming sessions are the corporate equivalent of recess. If your organization is serious about innovation then you must be serious about your approach. In the view of the authors you need to:

- Recruit for it
- Structure your organization for it and
- Nurture it every step of the way

More on these subjects in the chapters that follow.

Chapter 1 Key Learning

- Corporate Antibodies and Psychic Vampires are real. Expect them and be prepared to deal with them effectively and efficiently.
- Creative Voodoo is alive and well. Make certain that whatever "experts' your organization employs in the areas of creativity or innovation are held to the same high standards as every other discipline for which a consultant might be hired.
- Apply the same discipline, structure and hard work to brainstorming sessions as any other worthwhile endeavor.

Chapter Two –
What is Innovation anyway?

Good question.

It is important to explain that there is a big difference between innovation and creativity.   So let's start at the very beginning and consult the dictionary.

INNOVATION (noun) *the introduction of something new – new idea, new method or new device.*

INNOVATIVE (adjective) *characterized by, tending to, or introducing innovations.*

INNOVATE (verb) – *1. to introduce as if new 2. to make changes: do something in a new way.*

CREATIVITY (noun) *1. the quality of being creative and 2. the ability to create.*

CREATIVE (adjective) as *having the quality of something created rather than imitated.*

CREATE (verb) *1. To bring into existence 2. to produce through imaginative skill (e.g. a painting)*

That's what Webster says.

Here is what my incredibly practical wife said when I asked her - "Lisa, what is the difference between innovation and creativity?" (keep in mind that Lisa was a Creative Director for a major corporation - ☺). Her answer, (after a lengthy pause), "Hmmmmmmm... tough question. The difference is that innovation is something 'new new'".

Actually, she hit it on the head. Innovation is indeed that which is "new new". Notice how many times the word "new" is mentioned in Webster's definition of innovation.

Here's another way of looking at it. Innovation is the end result of something that is truly new or breakthrough in nature <u>and</u> that can be commercialized for profit.

That is what this book is really all about – nurturing innovation that leads to commercial value.

Examples: Henry Ford's assembly line, CD ROMs, DVDs, and mobile phones were innovative. They were not only innovative - they were also extraordinarily profitable. Entire industries were built on them. <u>The Power to Innovate</u> is not about being "creative" per se, or creating something, for its own sake.

A good friend of mine is president of a very successful promotions firm. In a very real sense he is in the "creativity business" just like an ad agency. For him innovation = *applied* creativity (i.e. creativity for its own sake does him no good – it's only in the harnessing of creativity *that someone is willing to <u>pay you</u> for that value is added*).

This book is about harnessing the process that leads to innovative breakthrough that can be leveraged for profit – whatever your business or vocation.

Practical business innovation - not art

Innovation, by nature, differs from creativity in that it is inherently tangible, practical and useful. And people are willing to pay you for it.

So how again is innovation different from creativity? There is a big difference. Creativity is the unique end result of human expression. Take

18

finger painting for example. A two year old can create some incredible finger painting. I still have the "elephant" that my son Robbie painted hanging on the bulletin board in my office. It is so creative. You should see it. Once I point out to my friends where the elephant is, and how my son has depicted it, they are amazed. I'm still amazed. Robbie's elephant, although priceless to me, has no commercial value. Finger painting is not innovative. That technique has been around as long as there has been paint and little fingers.

Think of Innovation and Creativity as two circles that slightly overlap. The circle with the dollar sign in it represents innovation. The circle with the paintbrush in it represents art – or creativity for its own sake. This book is all about the circle with the dollar sign in it.

What about the overlap area? On special occasions, creativity and innovation overlap. This is an intriguing area, relatively high profile and at the same time comparatively small. What makes you *want* that new dress, new car, or even that new blender? It's more likely than not, more than the fabric, horsepower or features - it's the feel, shape or color. This overlap area is where industrial design and fashion live. I call this area "commercialized art". Successful performing artists fall into this overlap area as well. Starving artists, finger painters, and Michael Jordan and Faith Hill hopefuls are in the circle with the paintbrush.

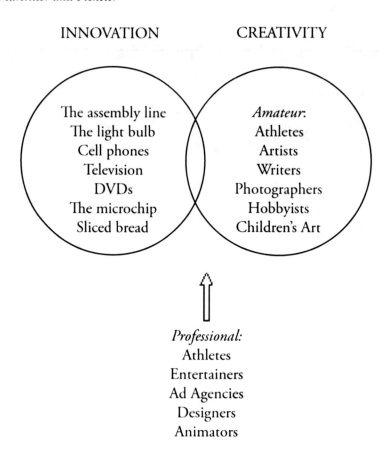

INNOVATION   CREATIVITY

The assembly line
The light bulb
Cell phones
Television
DVDs
The microchip
Sliced bread

Amateur:
Athletes
Artists
Writers
Photographers
Hobbyists
Children's Art

Professional:
Athletes
Entertainers
Ad Agencies
Designers
Animators

Think about Vincent van Gogh for example. Where would you put him and his art? Van Gogh is my favorite artist. His work, and technique was bold and truly breakthrough. Although influenced by the Impressionists, no one had ever painted like van Gogh before. He saw things that no one had ever seen and did things with a brush that no one had ever done. His technique, and art, was innovative. Did it have commercial value? Well, yes and no. Not in his lifetime anyway. His paintings barely kept him fed and he died in an asylum. You know the story. *But* almost 100 years after his death, one of his paintings; "Irises", sold at auction for over $40 million dollars. Of course in business, you don't have 100 years to wait for your return on investment.

Here are some questions to ponder.

- If you are in business, is your ad agency, or your <u>fill-in-the-blank agency</u>, creating art - *or* are they leveraging creativity to drive sales and build the equity of your brands?
- Is your R&D investment leading to commercialization or is some of it being used to find "the answer" for personal curiosity sake?
- Is the end result of your consumer research – "we need to do more research"?

Are you sure about your answers? Think hard about the human factors that drive individuals into fields such as art, science, or research in the first place. It is natural for scientists to fall in love with science for its own sake.

The answers to these questions are important. They represent the difference between the two circles – the difference between <u>innovating and creating art</u> – or the difference between <u>business and academia</u> – and ultimately the difference between <u>winning and losing</u>. Business people know that you have to compete and win and make a profit - right now. In the real world not everyone gets a trophy.

<u>The word INNOVATION is sure getting thrown around a lot.</u>

Is the word "innovation" prominently displayed in your company's mission statement or some other key company document? Very likely it is. Businesses today realize that there is nothing more important than out-innovating your competition. Innovation may be the final frontier of business advantage.

Let's reflect briefly on why this is so. The metamorphosis that business has undergone over the past 20 years has been remarkable and the value of companies has surged. At the expense of oversimplification, let me suggest that American business is evolving through four stages:

- Stage 1: "The Formula"
- Stage 2: The Learning Organization
- Stage 3: Cost Cutting
- Stage 4: Innovation

Historical Perspective:
Stage 1 "The Formula"

In stage 1 the focus is on ***generating*** demand. The Formula loosely describes how American business from the early 80's through the early 90's went about doing this. Although, my perspective was formed largely through my experiences in the consumer packaged goods industry, similar dynamics were in play across many industries.

In this stage we thought that our business and our strategies were quite sophisticated. In retrospect it was easy. Maybe it was too easy.

- The information and technology age hadn't kicked in yet
- Inflation was barreling along
- Advertising worked (really worked)
- Businesses had pricing power (i.e. prices could be raised without customers revolting)

It seemed like business was reduced to a formula, a formula that resulted in increased consumer demand. In many cases this is what that formula looked like for the top companies.

- Hire the best candidates out of the best schools – MBA's mandatory.
- Plug them into the business as "brand managers" – veritable general managers or mini-presidents for each of the company's products.
- Have them identify what consumers really wanted and then have them write "strategic marketing plans"
- Get your message out to the consumer - primarily via television advertising
- Take a price increase
- Watch the dollars come rolling in

Looking back, everything seemed so easy.

Maybe we were all overconfident?

- The stock market was coming out of 15 years of mediocre performance and was roaring to go.
- Consumer confidence was beginning to escalate
- Household spending power dramatically increased due to more females in the workforce than ever before. Remember DINKs? Dual Income No Kids.
- Inflation was growing at a high single digit rate.
- About five television channels represented 80% of our viewing and there were 30 and 60 second commercials. In 2004, the average household has 82 channels and viewers are exposed to 120 commercials during three hours of prime time viewing[1].

Under these circumstances, how could we *not* grow? It seemed like all the plans were working – and there was a reason for this. It was like placing a toy boat in a swiftly flowing stream. It was going to move. However, when the flow of the stream slowed down in the mid-90's things got a lot harder.

Stage 2: The Learning Organization

The Learning Organization focuses on learning faster than the competition and attaining competitive advantage as a result. The learning organization was all-the-buzz in the early 90's and companies invested heavily in it.

Perhaps nobody has received more accolades for their work with the concept of the Learning Organization than Peter Senge. In his breakthrough book, The 5th Discipline, Senge articulates the competitive advantages that accompany an organization's ability to learn faster than its competition. Senge stated that, "The only sustainable competitive advantage is to learn faster than the competition[2]".

In a nutshell, the concept of the Organizational Learning is characterized as follows.

- To thrive, organizations must assume responsibility for the ongoing learning of its employees to maintain competitive advantage.

- The employee must understand that learning doesn't end with graduate school (i.e. learning is perpetual)
- The importance of the organization's ability to learn will need to accelerate as society and technology become more complex and fast-paced.

These precepts are so well documented, and are now so intuitive, that they are accepted as being self-evident.

Of course it is also widely known that <u>enormous amounts of money</u> have poured into training and technology to enable the learning organization vision. There is also no doubt that these investments will continue into the future as they now basic to business success.

On a closely related front, it is important to note that *employee empowerment*, is also central to achieving long-term competitive advantage. Again, this area is so well documented and published, in both academia and the popular business press as to be considered self-evident. To underscore this point, Daft$_3$ (1998) notes that rapid change and global competition account for *a paradigm shift from traditional hierarchical management to the participative management structures so characteristic of postmodern management thinking. An outcropping of this shift is an increased need for interdependence, and a corresponding change in the role of managers from that of controlling employees to enabling or creating learning capability.* This capacity to learn is not intended to replace financial, marketing, and technological capabilities, rather to serve as the linchpin among them. Daft, like Senge, contends that learning faster than the competition may be the only remaining source of sustainable competitive advantage.

Stage 3: Cost Cutting

After "the formula" ran out of steam and organizations invested to become learning organizations, the financial guys stepped in. They reasoned, very rationally, that every dollar saved goes right to the profit bottom line. Of course this makes perfect sense. A penny saved is a penny earned. Or, to quote Andrew Tobias, "a penny saved can equal two pennies earned depending on your tax bracket".

From the mid-nineties onward there was an incredible emphasis on cost-savings and several areas received special attention.

Supply Chain - Wal*Mart taught the world the power of an efficient supply chain. Companies everywhere reaped enormous cost savings in their distribution systems.

Globalization – Suddenly, everyone realized "Holy cow, there are actually markets outside of the United States!" Where there was low-hanging fruit to be picked, new markets were opened up. It was fashionable to be global.

Acquisitions - The 90's through the early part of the 21st century were defined by acquisitions. Again, the rational made perfect sense. Big company buys little company and the duplicative parts – like the accounting, human resource and sales departments - are "rationalized". Costs are saved.

Outsourcing – This is sometimes referred to as off-shoring (i.e. turn your customer service department over to a firm in India that can do it cheaper).

Of course, cost cutting is as necessary as healthy cash flow to a successful business. However, problems will inevitably arise if we take our eye off the ball. The ball, in this case, is generating consumer demand or driving TOP LINE growth. Eventually, cost-cutting efforts will reach diminishing returns. In a worse case scenario cost cutting can denigrate the quality of the product to the point where consumers will take notice and rebel. What is also true is that EVERYBODY is cutting costs. If everyone is doing it – like the learning organization – then it no longer becomes a source of competitive advantage. We are all just running harder to keep up with the Joneses.

Stage 4: Onward to True Innovation

But first, a quick recap:

- "The formula" no longer works, as it's outdated. –The days of riding on the wave of inflation are long gone. TV advertising, which was the backbone of many successful brands, has lost its ability to make an impact.
- Everybody is investing in organizational learning. This is good. We've invested millions, set up employee skills classes. We've all read the books. We're doing better. We are keeping up with the Joneses.
- Everybody is investing in technology at a frantic rate. However, the return on investment for all this technology is still unclear. Consider that we have the latest IT infrastructures, cell phones, PCs, lap top computers, pagers, and PDAs - but so does our competition. We are so wired! We are so efficient! But where does all *this* end? Are we just learning how to cram 12 hours of work into 10 so that we can now do 2 extra hours?! Where is the balance in all this? People are beginning to say ENOUGH!
- We have laid-off workers, trimmed the fat, and cut costs. The balance sheets look a little better, but at what cost? Are our employees more stressed than ever? Is true productivity sliding back? Are we really creating true shareholder value, or just propping up the books for the short term? Are we in a downward death-spiral of cutting costs, distressing employees, who then become less productive, thereby leading to more cuts?

Once you get all your people hired, wired, and trained, and you've cut costs, the challenge becomes out-innovating your competition. Now that we have one-minute managers, an empowered workforce, and a learning organization, now what? We have all read the same books and have gotten smarter, faster and better. We have tapped into the human potential to lead and be led. We have become wired, or become wireless as the case may be, with technology like never before. We have cut back and become more efficient. So why are earnings not more robust and why are shareholders barking at the board? There are a lot of answers here, but a lot of it comes down to innovation. True innovation. When we look at ourselves in the mirror, how truly innovative are the products we market? How excited are the shoppers about buying them? If the answer is "not too", then there is a problem.

All these circumstances collide at a very crucial time in American business as companies are frantically trying to differentiate themselves.

Where does this all end? It all boils down to innovation. INNOVATION IS THE SOLUTION.

Add value or die. Differentiate or die. **Innovate or die.**

Build:

- Innovative ideas
- Innovative products
- Innovative services

Consumers are not dumb. They recognize true innovation when they see it and will pay a premium for it. Remember when Apple's IPOD music players first came out? People had them back-ordered for weeks. You couldn't get one unless you had a friend that worked in an Apple store. What was the advertising campaign that drove this demand? It was word of mouth. A highly innovative product that meets a consumer need goes a long way towards selling itself. Innovation drove that success.

In some cases it means getting back to what made companies great in the first place. It was often an innovation from 50 or 100 years ago that companies have been milking for decades. Where is that innovative spirit now?

It is obvious that innovation is terribly important. The question is what processes are in place for nurturing it in your company? Specifically:

- How do you get the maximum return on investment for all of that high-priced talent you have hired? What is your process?

- How do you make certain that you are hiring innovative people in the first place?
- Can you measure the innovation in your organization, establish a baseline and improve?
- How can you improve group dynamics so that the outcome is truly innovative vs. simply rehashing the same old ideas?
- How do you get the maximum return on investment for all the money you are spending in R&D?
- How do you leverage innovation to stay a step ahead of the competition?
- How can you produce or change the culture of your organization to be more innovative?

To summarize, <u>The Power to Innovate</u> is not about creativity for its own sake. It's not about finding answers for the sake of knowledge or creating art.

This book is about:

- Gaining, and sustaining competitive advantage.
- Creating a culture that allows innovation to occur.
- Leveraging innovation for profit

Business has everything to do with competition. In a best-case scenario, you will have re-written the rules and created an uneven playing field where you have an unfair competitive advantage. In other words, you'll have a better mousetrap.

The key question becomes, how well are you identifying, nurturing, and leveraging your innovation-based assets? The answer lies in understanding that all innovation follows a process.

Chapter Three – The Four Pillars of Innovation

An Overview

Innovation can be thought of as being built on four basic pillars which are undeniable. They are supported by fact including the latest scientific literature and research. They are further verified by the examples of innovative breakthroughs found throughout history: in business, science, technology, and in your own life and work place. They stand up to any measure of scrutiny including the test of time. These pillars are absolutely the foundation of the process by which innovation occurs. They work interdependently with each other, and if <u>any one of the pillars is missing</u>, INNOVATION CANNOT OCCUR.

THE FOUR PILLARS OF INNOVATION ARE:

- **Perseverance**
- **Knowledge**
- **Risk**
- **Passion**

The next five chapters are dedicated to bringing these pillars to life. You will be exposed to definitions, principles, examples, rationale, and scientific facts. You will also quickly learn *how* the pillars drive innovation. Equally important, you will not be exposed to half-baked theories, superficial antecdotes that insult your intelligence, or "voodoo solutions" to your real problems.

In *this* chapter, you will become more familiar with these pillars and the general role they play in innovation. In subsequent chapters, each pillar will be examined in detail and you will learn why they are so profound.

As was stated earlier, if any one of the pillars is missing, true innovation, *cannot* occur. <u>This is a profound statement</u> - profound in its simplicity. Einstein said, "Everything should be as simple as possible and not simpler". It's easy to make things more complicated.

It is profound because if **YOU UNDERSTAND THE VARIABLES TO INNOVATION, YOU CAN:**

- **IDENTIFY IT**
- **NURTURE IT**
- **LEVERAGE IT TO COMPETITIVE ADVANTAGE.**

This is at the core of what makes *The Power to Innovate* both breakthrough and unique.

The best way to truly understand the power of the four pillars is through real life examples that are self-evident. Through these examples, you will come to discover the indispensable role that Perseverance, Knowledge, Risk, and Passion play in innovation breakthroughs. Importantly, you will also come to understand that these pillars are hardwired into the attitudinal makeup of the innovator.

Throughout this book you will hear what the experts have to say. In this chapter, an incredible story will be shared which will bring to light the role of the four pillars.

The first story in Chapter 3 would go under the Jeopardy category, "Great innovators that nobody has ever heard of". In this case, the "answer is" – Charles Momsen (Admiral U.S. Navy). Sure, we could have told the stories of Sam Walton, Alexander Graham Bell, Thomas Edison, Bill Gates, or Steve Jobs. Huge industries were founded on their innovations. They are among the innovation giants. At the same time, you are probably already pretty familiar with what they did. By presenting a fresh story though, you will be engaged, entertained, and will learn. This first story will be told in some detail and will be referred to throughout the rest of the book. The second story in this chapter is familiar to everyone unless you live on the moon.

A Drama Not Invented in Hollywood

Our first story is not only incredible because of the innovation itself, but because of the sheer human drama. It is also a bit atypical, in that few people are aware of this wonderful man and his contributions. This story is also about the saving of human lives under the most perilous circumstances imaginable$_4$. This is the story of the U.S.S. Squalus, a submarine, and her sailors - sailors that certainly would have perished if it were not for the incredible Perseverance, Knowledge, Risk-taking, and Passion of one man. This man changed naval history.

When you think about a submarine, what comes to mind? Powerful? Claustrophobic? Scary? Exciting? Risky? Have you ever been onboard a submarine? Not many of us have.

Although I was only seven years old, I remember vividly the time that my father and I boarded an submarine docked in Baltimore Harbor. It was an old WW II sub that had become a tourist attraction. It was definitely out of commission. I have long since forgotten her name. I do remember though that it was light gray. It was pretty stark and it didn't have any guns on it or other cool stuff I was hoping it might have. I remember going down the hatch. It was amazing inside. Not like I thought it might be – maybe a playhouse or something. No. I recall that the inside was nothing like I had ever experienced before. Everything seemed to be made of steel - everything was hard. It was kind of dark and it smelled bad. This was not a comfortable place. This was a functional place, and a cramped place, and a scary place to a seven year old. I remember climbing out of the hatch and seeing the blue sky. I was glad to be out of that thing!

These images came pouring back to me as I read the book *The Terrible Hours*₅. This New York Times #1 bestseller, by Peter Mass is <u>a must read</u>, but not for the faint-hearted. I highly recommend that you buy this book. You might recall that Peter Mass also wrote *Underboss*, *The Valachi Papers*, *Serpico*, and *Manhunt* among others.

The book chronicles the ordeal of the U.S.S. Squalus, a submarine that sunk on her maiden voyage off the coast of New England in May of 1939. A faulty valve let the seawater pour in and she sank like a rock in almost 300 feet of water. All 59 crewmembers were trapped on board. They had been able to seal off the section of the sub where the water poured in but they were solidly stuck on the bottom of the ocean. As my seven year old Robbie would say, "this is not good".

Not only was this not good; it was a death sentence. A horrible death sentence. Up unto that point, no one had ever survived a submarine sinking in more than 50 feet of water. The bottom line was this – if you went down in a submarine, you were a goner. Period. This is something that submariners accepted. In fact, it was pointedly avoided, so much so that it was taboo even to discuss the subject.

There is no possible way to escape alive if the water is more than about 50 feet deep even if the hatch could be opened (which at that point is impossible anyway because of the tons of ocean water pressing against it). But even if you could open the hatch the pressure of the ocean would wreak havoc with your body. Specifically, your lungs and the air within them would change dramatically under the pressure and your blood chemistry would rapidly change. You would either drown, your own air becomes toxic, or you experience an excruciating and lethal attack of "the bends". So at *300 feet* - forget it. These men trapped on board - alive and with less than 3 days air supply, were simply doomed. And they knew it. Can you imagine a more awful fate? Think about it. Or if you are more like my wife Lisa – "no honey, I really don't want to think about it".

So what does all this have to do with Perseverance, Knowledge, Risk and Passion? It has everything to do with them! Because these trapped sailors didn't die. They didn't die because of one man. This man was Charles Bowers Momsen. Everyone called him "Swede". To quote Peter Mass, "many would say he was the greatest submariner the Navy ever had........an extraordinary combination of visionary, scientist and man of action"

Let's learn more about this man and what made him tick. Swede Momsen's career as a Navy man was almost over before it began. Momsen entered Annapolis in 1914. In the spring of his freshman year, a cheating scandal was exposed at the Naval Academy and the exams the following fall term were made doubly difficult. In the wake of this (pun intended), more than 300 midshipmen failed and had to resign. One of them was Momsen.

He did not give up though. Instead, he quickly tried for reappointment from his home district congressman in St. Paul Minnesota. The odds were stacked against him – and then it got worse. The Republican, who originally sponsored him was no longer in office, *and* had lost his seat to a Democrat! This is not good! Momsen continued though to doggedly pursue his career with the new Democratic representative, Carl Van Dyke. Finally Van Dyke surrendered, specifying in a letter to Momsen's father why he had done so. "I want to make it perfectly clear that the only reason for my reappointing your son, Charles, is because of Charles himself". In other words, he was saying, I'd rather eat worms than support a Republican, but I believe in your son.

Momsen graduated from Annapolis in 1919 on an accelerated schedule brought on by WWI and was commissioned an ensign aboard the Battleship *Oklahoma*. The Oklahoma was one of the Navy's flagships. However, after only two years with the *Oklahoma*, Momsen was bored and sought something more exciting.

In 1921, he got the opportunity he wanted and applied for submarine school in New London, Connecticut. The captain of the *Oklahoma* took him aside. "I think you've got a bright future," he counseled. "Better reconsider. Only the scum of the Navy go into pigboats (i.e. subs)". The Oklahoma's captain wasn't unique. The Navy's pride was in the big battleships. Submarines, on the other hand, were grudgingly tolerated as new sea weapons (and weapons in a kind of underhanded way when you got right down to it). Certainly these subs were not the place for a proper, career-oriented, young officer. An Annapolis man faced double jeopardy. He not only had to face the enormous risks involved with submarines, but also the social risks associated with going against the norm of Navy society.

In spite of the risks Momsen loved his life as a submariner. It was onboard his first command, the O-15 however, that he had his first, harrowing, near-death, experience. While under full power, the sub was ordered to dive. The diving planes however, become stuck and the sub continued to dive downward until it was too late! The O-15 struck the ocean floor and had literally become stuck in the mud. Only by carefully blasting water out of his torpedo-tubes doors a series of times was the O-15 finally able to free herself from the muck. It floated free. Momsen and his crew had survived. Barely. These happy endings were few and far between.

In 1925 for example, the submarine S-51, was not so lucky. On a moonless night, the S-51 collided with a passenger ship and sank. Momsen got the news at 3:00 AM and was ordered to get his sub underway and join the search and rescue mission. This was personal. The S-51 was in his division, a sister sub. Her officers were personal friends, classmates from Annapolis.

When his sub got to the spot, then marked by a buoy, there was nothing. It was Momsen himself, then commanding the S-1, who found her telltale oil slick and the bubbles rising from her hull 130 feet down. There was nothing that could be done. The sense of futility was overwhelming. Recalling the scene, Momsen wrote, "we tried to contact her but there was only silence in return. Those of us on the bridge simply stared into the water and said nothing. No one at that time knew anything about the principles of rescue. We were utterly helpless. I've never felt more utterly useless".

He would recall something else too. Months later, when the sub had been raised, he would witness the horribly contorted faces of those who didn't drown right away. Many of these, including a close friend, Jim Haselden, also had flesh-shredded fingers as they tried to claw their way out of their steel coffin.

Haselden's face haunted his dreams night after night and anger grew within in him. Surely there must be some means to save submariners like Haselden, or at least give them a fighting chance. For weeks Momsen wrestled with that problem. Finally, an idea began to take place. The idea was simple. A large, steel, rescue chamber, resembling a bell, would be lowered from the surface via cables and would be bolted over the submarine's escape hatch. Once bolted in place and the hatch opened, the rescuers would be able to go down into the submarines compartments or the trapped men would be able to crawl out on their own.

Momsen hashed over the plans and the idea obsessively. He shared it freely with his fellow submarine skippers. Nobody could find fault with it. He then committed his idea to paper in great detail and took it to the submarine base commander who said, "Swede, I think you've got a hell of an idea here".

The Commander then forwarded the plan to the Navy's Bureau of Construction and Repair for an expert appraisal. This same commander personally endorsed the plan. No response came back. At first, this didn't bother Momsen. But the weeks turned into months and the then the months into a year. Still no response. Perhaps they had found a major flaw in the design? He feared the worst and had already begun to turn over another escape device in his mind. Then he found out. And in a way that he never could have expected.

He was due for a tour of shore duty and found out that he had been transferred to none other than the Navy's Bureau of Construction and Repair! Still upset by the lack of a response, he couldn't help but wonder if there was a connection. When he reported in however, nobody knew anything about a rescue chamber. During his very first day he had the opportunity to go through a pile of "awaiting action" papers that his predecessor had left behind.

He was dumbfounded. There at the bottom of the stack was his proposed design, including the Commander's endorsement – the whole works!! Nothing had been done with it. He was angry beyond words.

By morning he had pulled himself together as much as he could and began pleading his case throughout the bureau. The response? Very cold.

- "Who the hell" was this new lieutenant?
- Already two days on the job and he is pushing some screwball idea to get people out of submarines!
- His idea to boot!
- You'd think he was the first person to ever think of that problem? The bureau had been fooling around with it for years....

Momsen persisted, but it was no use. His proposal was dumped back on his desk with the note, "impractical from the standpoint of seamanship". Even this he furiously protested. The matter, he was informed, was "closed".

Tragically, within weeks of his final turndown, another submarine went down off the coast of Cape Cod. In Washington, Momsen read the telegrams as her crew slowly asphyxiated. One of the last messages tapped out by the doomed men was an impossible request, "please hurry".

The headlines touched off a national uproar. Thousands of letters were sent into the Navy Department. Get rid of submarines! Others demanded a way to save such men. As the Navy's brass thought about what to do next, some of the letters, calling for an investigation, had been forward to him by Congress. This was almost more than he could stand. All the while he possessed the bitter knowledge that his rescue chamber could have made the difference.

He would not be denied. As the letters came across his desk he began to consider another idea that he had been thinking about during his long wait--an idea completely different from the rescue chamber. This time however, no official sanction would be required. No. This time Momsen determined that he would not go through official Navy channels again.

Instead he sought smart, free-spirited engineers, to help him. Some of them were civilians. So with a handful of volunteers to assist him, he tackled with renewed determination, the designing, the building, and the testing of his devices. These included not only the rescue chamber, but a new device, which men trapped in a sub, could use to "breathe" as they rose to the surface.

At this point in the story, it is important to note that very little was known about diving at depths greater than 100 feet. The changes in body chemistry that took place at ocean depths were almost a complete mystery. This was a daunting task for Momsen and his team. Probing a world without funds, operating almost alone, buoyed only by his belief in himself. He was determined not to be denied.

Over the course of the next several years, Momsen experimented with different mixtures of "air" that could sustain divers at various depths. Using this experimental tank, and his volunteer divers and doctors, Momsen was able to put together the combinations of Oxygen, Nitrogen and Helium that would be needed to enable human life at various depths. He painstakingly began to unravel the mystery of poisonous carbon monoxide build-up (a by-product of exhaling) and how to counter it. His work was revolutionary and breakthrough - and also low profile.

The second device that he developed was a special breathing apparatus that later became known as the "Momsen lung". Based on his years of experimentation, and using only basic materials, he was able to create a self-contained breathing device. Similar to a life jacket, the "lung" would allow a person to rise to the surface via breathing through a tube without experiencing a deadly attack of the bends. If a sailor could get out of a submarine in less than 110 feet of water (the same depth the S-51 had gone down in), this lung could save his life.

By using his pressure tank and through endless experimentation, Momsen's devices began to come to reality. His team began to figure out the correct air mixtures to sustain the rescue chamber at various depths and make the Momsen lung work. His first breakthroughs began in 1928 when he successfully sustained his divers in simulated depths of 100, 200, and 300 feet.

Interestingly, at this same time, word had begun to spread around that Momsen was fooling around with some sort of escape devices. Nobody within the Navy took them seriously. After all, the best engineering minds in the Navy had been called in after the S-4 tragedy and nothing was even off the drawing board.

It was at this point that Momsen decided that he needed to conduct a dramatic demonstration. He decided to demonstrate what his lung could do. He chose a hole in the Potomac River, in Washington D.C., that was 110 feet deep. This was intensely dangerous. The water was muddy and the current made the situation worse. But as fate would have it that day, he not only survived, but his lung worked. His team was ecstatic!

He also got a big boost from an unexpected source. About half way through the experiment a young man began waving frantically from the bank. He was so persistent that Momsen finally sent over a small boat to pick him up. He turned out to be a "cub reporter", one A.W. Gilliam, from the Washington Star. The boat brought him back to meet Momsen. What happened next was pure genius. Momsen allowed the youngster to not only witness his ascent, but allowed the young man to experience the sensation of an ascent from about 20 feet himself. Gilliam hurried back to the Washington Star with the scoop of a lifetime!

The Navy brass found out about what had happened on the Potomac like everybody else – by reading the paper! The next day when Momsen's diving boat returned to Washington, a notable collection of Navy brass, some with red faces, were there to greet him. Were they thrilled that Momsen had made a breakthrough that could save the lives of their fellow sailors!? Ah, no. The Chief of Naval Operations, Admiral Charles Hughes, who was personally on hand to meet the boat, spoke for all of the brass when he demanded of Momsen, "Young man, what the hell have you been up to?"

The word though was out. The news made headlines across the nation and the Navy, of course, quickly approved more tests. Swede now had the staff and the budget he needed to accelerate his experimentation and perfect his devices.

His next major demonstration came off the coast of Florida in 1929. At that time, Momsen and his team used the resurrected S-4 as an experiment station. The experiment was a bold one and ingenious. In one of the compartments to be flooded, the motor room, Momsen installed a steel "skirt ". The idea was to get the crew out of the sub by first unlocking the hatch cover and then letting the sea in through the flood valves. As the water came in, it would compress the air in the compartment until the hatch was forced open (i.e. blown off). After the water level rose above the lower edge of the skirt, the external and internal pressure would equilibrate, leaving an air pocket. It would be in this air pocket that the crew would don their lungs before rising to the surface through the now-open hatch. This all looked good on paper of course, but they wouldn't know it would actually work until they tried.

They sunk this S-4 laboratory in 100 feet of water off of Key West. Momsen and another diver, Ed Kalinsoki, descended down to the sunken sub. Once on board the sub, they opened the flood valves according to plan. The water rushed in until the air pressure in the top of the sub equaled that of the water pressure inside the hull. At this point the water was almost head-high. A bit higher than was calculated! At this point Kolinoski said, "Mr. Momsen, I hope to Christ, you know what you are doing!" They couldn't have simulated actual disaster conditions any better! With an enormous crash, the hatch blew off and the pressure equalized in their compartment, exactly as planned. They then put on their breathing lungs and slowly and carefully ascended to the surface ("staying in the air bubbles to avoid any possible sharks"). Only 14 months before, eight men had died with no chance in the same motor room from which they had just exiting. This event made headline news and the Navy was now basking in the glow created by Momsen.

Swede wasn't finished however. Not even close. He now wanted to try the same approach but only deeper. He next repeated the escape from 207 feet, at a depth that no human had ever ascended without a diving helmet. He repeated the feat – this time at night. All went well and history was made again.

"Well done" messages poured in from the White House and elsewhere. This time the Navy, instead of cursing Momsen, awarded him the Distinguished Service Medal. "Lieutenant Momsen, repeatedly and voluntarily risked his own life in conducting experiments of a nature such that there was little or no information available as to their probable results...... It is through his initiative, courage and perseverance..... That the development of the lung reached its successful conclusion."

But more important to Swede Momsen was the announcement from the Secretary of the Navy that contracts had been established for seven thousand lungs. Additionally, every new sub would now have Momsen's escape hatches and the 75 submarines already in existence would be retrofitted.

Over the next decade, Swede Momsen and his crew experimented and then perfected the lungs and the escape chamber device. They perfected them in practice at least, but never in a real maritime disaster. Never, that is until the Squalus went down on that fateful day in May 1939.

What happened next was truly astounding, heroic and history making. Hollywood could not have concocted such a story, but perhaps they should!

You already know that the Squalus went down in 300 feet of water off the coast of New England, near Portsmouth New Hampshire. Here is an account of what happened. The day was May 23, 1939 and the Squalus was ready for her inaugural dive. In Navy time it was 08:30. Everything was looking good. All the lights that indicated shut valves changed from red to green exactly like they were supposed to and all was in order. They began to descend deeper and deeper.

Suddenly the submarine began to shake and a voice from the engine compartment shouted out– "the compartment is flooding!!" Everyone in the control was stunned - the indicator lights were still unaccountably green. This could not be happening!! But it was! A nightmare was unfolding in front of them. With terrifying force, tons of water were now pouring through the main diesel induction valves and shooting through the engine rooms like a thousand fire hoses! The next few seconds were like hours and there was complete chaos on board. Frantic attempts were made to blow ballast and return the ship to the surface, but it was too late. To the horror of all on board, they also had to seal the door to the engine compartment, even though there were still men back there, to avoid all of them drowning on the spot. The Squalus was going down into the dark sea. Down to the ocean floor. She hit the bottom with a thud and then the lights went out – all but the faint emergency lighting. She lay helpless in 243 feet of water. The temperature outside her hull was near freezing. Then things got worse.

- Her sinking was not noticed right away. Submarines were not always on time when reporting in. But when the minutes went by, and then that first hour, people started to worry. Then people began to fear the worst.
- Another submarine was then sent to try to find her. At noon though, its report brought only dismal news, "Have not sighted the Squalus, am calling her with sound gear (i.e. the predecessor of sonar)"
- They knew that the crew on board the Squalus had about 2 1/2 days air supply (max) and that poisonous Carbon Dioxide gas build-up was a real issue.
- The weather was rapidly turning foul, making rescue conditions perilous to impossible.
- The water was too deep and frigid to attempt to use Momsen's Lungs
- The nearest vessel containing one of Momsen's rescue chambers was the *Falcon*, and she was docked in New London, Connecticut. There were only five rescue chambers in existence and this was the only one remotely close enough.

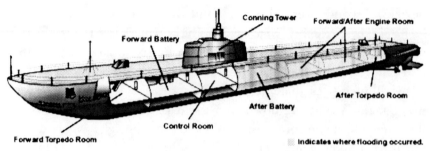

Diagram of Flooded USS Squalus: Courtesy of Office of Naval Research

This was the situation that Admiral Cyrus Cole, the commander of the Portsmouth Naval Yard, was assessing. It was at this point, that the Admiral put the call into Washington to the office of the Chief of Naval Operations. He outlined the uncertainty, its morbid possibilities, and then asked for the Falcon to be immediately sent to the site of the sinking. He also said, "And it's critical that we have Swede Momsen. We must have him. He's going to be the key to all this. He's gone off somewhere hasn't he?"

The response from Washington was "No, no, don't worry, he's with his diving unit" and then added, "And thank the good Lord that he never gave up".

At that moment, Swede Momsen was in the Washington Naval Yard with his diving team. One of his divers was in the middle of a simulated 250-foot dive using a new combination of gases including Helium and Oxygen.

The phone then rang and he figured it was likely the girlfriend of one of the divers. On the other end though was Commander Lockwood from Naval Operations. "Swede", he said, "there's hell to pay. The Squalus may be down. All indications are that she is and we are presuming the worst".

"How deep?"

"About 200 to 300 feet"

"There's no time to lose, there is a front moving in and the forecast is for dense fog". We're getting a plane ready for you now. Space for you and three others, we'll get the rest of your team there as fast as we can"

After 14 years the day had come. And despite the doubters, the politics, the backbiting and the skeptics, all his work, the long days and restless nights of dreaming and planning had been validated. He thought about how the Navy was controlled by battleship admirals and then recalled how one of them had sneered, "Who does this Momsen think he is, Jules Verne?"

The truth, of course, was that without him, there would be no hope for the crew of the Squalus. But none of his breakthrough work had ever been used in an actual catastrophe. And now they would be under the worst possible conditions – bad weather, frigid water, and the men terribly far down. By the end of the day, and against all odds though, the greatest undersea rescue of all time was in full swing.

By afternoon of that first day, the tension at the Portsmouth Yard and in Washington was almost unbearable. Then they got the word. A marker buoy from the Squalus had been found. While, this was good news, in that they knew where she had gone down, it was also devastating in that this confirmed their worst fears. The slender hope that somehow this was all a false alarm was now gone. Now more bad news– the cable from the marker buoy to the sub was actually severed. It was floating freely. They only new approximately where the Squalus was. Not only that, the cable was the guide the helmeted divers would need to get down to the sunken sub.

A small collection of rescue ships had been assembled, many of them old, and was headed towards the sub's location. Momsen and his team were in the air and on the way. The Falcon though, one of the oldest crafts, was also one of the slowest rescue ships and lagged painfully behind the others.

It took them almost all day just to find the Squalus on the ocean floor. The rescue boat, *Penacock*, tried to locate her with grappling hooks, but they proved too light and the sea too choppy. The weather reports were now calling for dense fog, which would only make things worse. They then tried to drag the bottom with the rescue ship's anchor.

43

To quote Peter Mass, "this exercise was roughly the same as trying to locate a pen which had been dropped from a 3rd story building with a piece of string and a bent pin – while blindfolded."

Meanwhile, down below on board the *Squalus*, the crew could hear the propellers of the Penacock, going back and forth over them – searching for them. Their air was becoming increasingly foul. Then at 1930 hours (7:30 PM), and in the growing darkness, the makeshift grapnel hook from the Penacock caught onto something and held. It was the Squalus. They had made contact.

The entire Nation was aware now of the plight of the Squalus. The press was eager for any news. The reality though was not good. The crew was very cold, it was near dark, their air was becoming increasingly foul and most of them were nauseous. But at least they had some limited communication. By tapping out words in Morse code with a hammer, the *Penacock* could discern their condition. The first message ordered, as much for the men as for the rescuers was, "Conditions satisfactory, but cold".

As day broke the following morning, the rescue operation began in earnest. The three-part plan was as follows:

1. Use Momsen's diving team (helmeted deep sea divers with their special air mixtures) to go down and attach cables to the sub.
2. Once the cables were attached, the 10-ton rescue chamber would be lowered and bolted in place over the hatch.
3. Air would then be pumped into the rescue chamber to equal the pressure in the Squalus, the hatch opened, and the men brought to the surface inside the chamber.

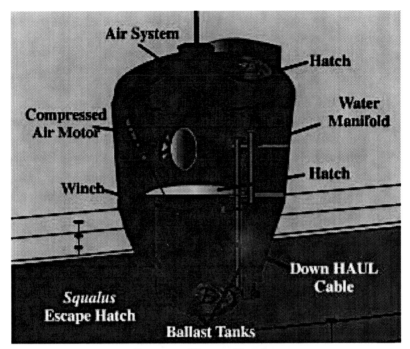

Diagram of Rescue Chamber

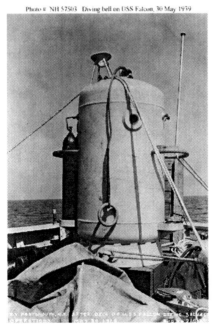

Rescue Chamber aboard the FALCON:
Courtesy of Office of Naval Research[6]

That was the plan. It was straightforward in design, but almost impossible to execute under the conditions.

There were many intense complications to be overcome to pull this off as follows.

- At this depth and pressure, divers get very disoriented and confused, almost like being drunk. Their judgment becomes impaired. Their EVERY move had to be monitored closely on the surface through communication microphones.
- Divers could not stay down for long. Just a few minutes at a time. It was intensely dangerous.
- The sea was frightfully cold, the diver suits, though heated, were very uncomfortable.
- The series of steel cables and air hoses to supply the divers were always dangerously close to becoming entangled. If they did, there would be almost certain death.
- The rescue chamber had never been used in an actual disaster. So they weren't sure it would work under these conditions.
- The weather got worse and the seas got higher and various lines got closer and closer together. A strong wind began to make the sea heave. The sea was not helping their efforts to save the crew.
- It took four hours just to get the four anchors of the *Falcon* in place over the presumed location of the sub.
- A Coast Guard Cutter full of reporters was close by waiting to relay the news to a nation that was anxiously waiting.
- At this point, every minute was critical.

It was in this environment that Momsen and his crew worked. Risking death on every dive, they repeatedly went back into the sea for the next eight hours. They kept going back down to the submarine until the rescue chamber was secured in place over the hatch.

At this point, Momsen, on board the *Falcon*, could hear the noise of the chamber being attached to the Squalus via his diver's communication microphone. In all this excitement he heard his diver report, "upper hatch is open, but no answer from the submarine". What? After all this, were they too late? No! The, skipper of the sub had ordered that the hatch escape area be shut off **until** he was certain all was in order. He now ordered that hatch open**ed**. The diver, John Mihalowski, looked down in the faint light, and he could distinguish the pale faces staring back up at him. It was then that Momsen heard the magic words, "Mihalowski sees them!! "When I heard that, Momsen later recalled, I experienced a thrill that I cannot possibly describe and I wonder if any man ever could".

Upon seeing the men, Mihalowski himself didn't know what to say. It was as if both he and the men below were rendered speechless. "Well", he finally said, "we're here. I'm handing down soup, coffee and sandwiches". One of the men replied, "what, no napkins?!" To say they were relieved and overjoyed beyond words would be the understatement of the 20th century!

The last part of the rescue was supposed to be relatively straightforward. Repeatedly lower the rescue chamber taking several sailors off the sub at a time until they were all rescued. What happened next though, sounds so much like Hollywood as to not be true – but is was true.

The skipper of the Squalus, Oliver Nanquin, decided who would get into the rescue chamber and be hoisted slowly to the surface, and who would stay. He chose two men who barely escaped the after battery compartment (the compartment that had to be quickly sealed off to prevent the entire sub from flooding) and five others that were suffering miserably from the cold. They were secured in the rescue chamber, the proper hatches were secured and ballast blown. This took about 15 minutes. Then very slowly the chamber began to rise as the motor reel winch mechanism on the chamber began to hoist them toward the surface.

Finally, the chamber was visible through the water, "like a great green blob" according to one reporter. It then broke the surface and was quickly secured on board the Falcon. Lieutenant Nichols was the first to stick his head up out of the rescue chamber. Cheers erupted on board and on the ships surrounding him. Nichols squinted in the sunlight and faltered as he tried to get out. Dozens of hands helped him got on deck. One by one the men exited the chamber! They all hugged Swede and had huge smiles.

With all the rejoicing though, there was also the sobering news that over 20 men had drowned – the ones did not make it out of the after battery compartment before it was sealed off. This information had to be relayed back to shore to the nerve-wracked wives, girlfriends, and family members.

But still, men had been saved in historic fashion. Things were going well. A little too well as it turned out. There were still many other men to get to the surface safely.

The second batch of crewman went much like the first except that they carried two more men this time. When the chamber emerged again on the surface, Momsen could see right away that the heavy seas were putting an enormous strain on the cable and winch equipment. He knew that nine survivors per trip was the maximum load. With 18 men left on board, two addition trips would be required – if the equipment would last. At this point though, the sky began to cloud again and the wind began to pick up. This change in weather could raise havoc with the rescue equipment if it continued.

The chamber went down the third time and collected another nine sailors. Maximum load. Everything went according to plan. As this group of survivors came on board the Falcon, the ordeal clearly showed on their weary faces. They were chilled to the bone and fatigued beyond description. For Momsen though it was a fantastic sight.

One last trip and they would have the last of the surviving crew. Each descent had taken about an hour and the round trip took slightly more than two. It would be dark before the last group was on board. Presently, the sea began to rise and it began to rain.

The rescue chamber was lowered one last time, secured to the hatch and the last survivors, eight of them, got inside. The ballast was blown and the chamber began to reel itself up. Then at 160 feet it happened. Over the phone, Momsen heard, "the cable is jammed on the reel, we're stuck". They tried several things to un-jam the cable but nothing worked. It was now getting dark.

They decided to lower the chamber back down to the bottom. The plan was for a diver to enter the water, go back down the rescue chamber and attach a "retrieving cable" that could be attached to the Falcon's winch system. Of course the old cable on the jammed reel had to be cut away by the diver with wire cutters. The fact that this was actually done under those conditions was Herculean in itself. But it was done.

Ever so slowly the chamber was winched to the surface. On the stern of the Falcon everyone watched the cable coming out of the sea under the huge floodlights. Suddenly, before their horrified eyes, they saw the strands of the retrieving wire had begun to unravel!! The strain was too great. It was coming apart! Stop the winch! Ever so slowly, they lowered the chamber to the bottom again and again sent yet another diver to put on another cable. Only this time it just couldn't be done. It was simply beyond the skill of the best divers in the world.

They were now out of options. They decided to lift the chamber slowly from the bottom and pray that the frayed cable didn't break. Momsen personally held the cable between his fingers as to gauge the strain on it. The winch operators would let out line and bring in line as the sea rose and fell. A sudden swell of the sea could easily break the cable. They had no choice. If the cable broke, all the men on board would perish. Slowly under the floodlights, they watched the cable come up inch at a time. Only a single strand of cable was left! Ever so slowly they worked that part out of the water and a deck hand was finally able to secure it with a clamp. The rest was simple and they were then able to winch the chamber on board. Their ordeal was over. It was 38 minutes past midnight, 39 hours since Squalus had sunk. The skipper, Oliver Naquin was the last helped on deck.

Rescued Sailors: Courtesy of Milne Special Collections and Archives
Department, University of New Hampshire Library, Durham, NH.

In Portsmouth, Hansen Baldwin, covering the story for the New York Times, wrote, "Man won a victory from the sea early this morning".

Swede Momsen continued to serve his country with a most distinguished career and retired as Vice Admiral in 1955.

Admiral Swede Momsen (Ret. USN): Courtesy of U.S. Naval Academy Archives

Momsen's Connection to the Four Pillars

What a great story! The truth is always more amazing than fiction. Do yourself a favor and get the book. It's dynamite – this brief paraphrasing does not capture the drama.

But what does this have to do with the four pillars of innovation? EVERYTHING! This story is a PERFECT EXAMPLE of innovation and the four pillars that <u>caused</u> it to happen.

Let's review in some detail beginning with two key questions.

- Was Swede Momsen being "Creative" or Innovative?
- Did he invent something that was "new, new" (i.e. truly innovate) or did he represent his personal expression of a technique that had already been around (i.e. creative)?

No question, what he did was INNOVATIVE. His work not only had "commercial value" (7,000 Momsen Lungs ordered and submarines equipped with the rescue chambers) but more importantly, his innovation saved lives. What he did was <u>*not*</u> creativity for creativity's sake.

To follow is a review of the role each of the pillars played throughout the drama.

1. RISK

Did Swede Momsen take risks? Yes, he took enormous risks.

- <u>Social risk</u> – Pigboats were not a proper place for an Annapolis graduate's career. And, "who does this Momsen think he is, Jules Verne?"
- <u>Personal Risk</u> – Being a submariner in the first place and oh yes - drowning, dying an excruciating death from the bends, dying from asphyxiation, diving into frigid seas at night or the muddy Potomac during the day. Remember the sharks? What else?

- <u>Financial risks</u> – There were certainly financial risks associated with his career decisions. Not too many people enter the Navy to strike it rich, so career and "toeing the line" are integral with compensation – particularly in the military. What about the fact that he basically had no funds to work with in his early career?
- What <u>other</u> risks did he take?

RISK, and its role in innovation, will be broken down further in chapter 6.

2. PERSEVERANCE

Did Swede Momsen exhibit PERSEVERANCE? Absolutely – and in copious amounts.

In review:

- Getting into Annapolis in the first place
- Getting readmitted to Annapolis with a different sponsor
- Going to Submarine school after a Navy Captain advised him not too
- Going back and pleading his case (i.e. the rescue chamber) to Naval Affairs after it had been officially "closed"
- Going around the official system in pursuit of his vision
- Putting up with the politics, backbiting and small mindedness of nay Sayers.
- 14 years of experimenting with various air mixtures and new escape devices (under real and simulated conditions).
- In the case of the Squalus rescue, over 39 hours of mind numbing tension, cold and choppy seas.
- Bottom line: He could have given up SO MANY times, but did not.
- In what other ways did Momsen persevere?

The role that Perseverance plays in the innovation process is detailed in Chapter 4.

What special KNOWLEDGE did Momsen have that allowed him to succeed?

3. KNOWLEDGE

- Nobody on earth knew more about underwater rescue than Swede Momsen.
- Nobody knew more about air mixtures and their effect on humans in deep water than Momsen.
- He had firsthand experience as a submariner.
- He was an Annapolis graduate and his curriculum included heavy doses of leadership and engineering.
- He had the knowledge, and wisdom, of how to get the most out of others and be sensitive to what they were communicating to him.
- In what other areas did Momsen have special knowledge or leverage his knowledge?

KNOWLEDGE will be examined in detail in chapter 5.

Did Swede Momsen have passion? Yes, in abundance.

4. PASSION

- He saw firsthand, the horrible scenes where submarines had gone down and experienced the absolute frustration of knowing that there was nothing he could do.
- He learned of the contorted, lifeless face of a friend, who had died in a submarine sinking.
- He saw the shredded fingers of men who had unsuccessfully tried to claw their way out of a sunken sub.
- He had many restless nights turning over in his mind how an escape device might be like
- Could he have taken all those risks without passion?
- Could he have persevered without passion?
- In what other ways did Swede Momsen demonstrate passion?
- Is passion the most important of all the pillars?

The unique role that PASSION plays in the innovation process will be detailed in chapter 7.

CHAPTER SUMMARY

The four pillars of innovation were highly visible in this extraordinary story. Not only were they visible, they were also interrelated. So much so that the story and the innovation never would have occurred if any one of them was missing. That is a powerful statement.

- Could Momsen have saved those men if he didn't persevere? NO.
- Could Momsen have saved those men if he didn't have special knowledge? NO
- Could Momsen have saved those men if he didn't take risks? NO.
- Could Momsen have saved those men if he didn't have passion? NO.
- Could Momsen have saved those men if he was lacking any one of these? NO.

Consider the following:
- Did all of this happen by accident? No.
- It happened *by design and by a process.*
- By the process that is inherent (and self-evident) in the four pillars.

Think about any great innovation in the last 100 years. Now describe how the four Pillars were integral to that innovation coming to life.

This list will get you started.

- Albert Einstein and the Manhattan Project and first atomic bomb.
- Henry Ford and the Assembly Line.
- The Apollo Space Program and getting those men back alive on Apollo 13.

- Larry Ellison and Oracle (read the book The Proving Ground)
- Steve Jobs of Apple and Pixar Studios fame (How incredible was the movie <u>The Incredibles?</u> – setting the standard for digital animation while delivering a superior product)
- Burt Rutan and his crew for winning the X Prize for space travel.

Upon further reflection, it is evident that the four pillars are integral in all areas where innovation occurs. In business, in the military, in politics, and in <u>*your personal life*</u> as well.

Wherever there is breakthrough INNOVATION you will find the four pillars working as part of the process.

The Four Pillars of Innovation and Jesus??

To illustrate just how universal and self-evident the principles of innovation are, consider for a moment the life of Jesus. I'm not preaching here, just making a point about the pillars being self-evident.

- Did Jesus change the world? Yes. Time is split between those things that happened before and after His birth. It could accurately be said that He changed the entire notion of "religion" and man's relationship with God. That just might be the ultimate innovation.

Consider the following:

- Did Jesus take **risks**? Yes. Specifically, He took <u>unfathomable and unprecedented</u> personal, social and religious risks.
- Did Jesus **persevere**? Yes. Through death.
- Did Jesus have **knowledge**? Yes. Believers would say He literally knows *ALL* things (including the number of hairs on your head, grains of sand on the beach, and how He knows you better than you know yourself). Even non-believers must be impressed with how Jesus quoted over 20 different books and over 100 different passages from the Old Testament during his ministry. Even as a boy, His <u>knowledge</u> and comprehension

of the written religious word was unprecedented and, "the scholars in the temple were amazed"

- Did Jesus have **passion**? Did anyone ever have more? The movie the <u>Passion of Christ</u> comes to mind.

Chapter 3 Key Learning

1. Meaningful Innovation <u>doesn't happen by accident.</u>
2. <u>Innovation</u> happens as a result of a process (whether the innovator knows it or not)
3. The process, inherent in the 4 pillars, is universal.

Chapter Four – Perseverance

"Genius is 1% inspiration and 99% perspiration"
Thomas Edison

"Nothing in this world can take the place of persistence. Talent will not; nothing is more common than unsuccessful men with talent. Genius will not; un-rewarded genius is almost a proverb. Education will not; the world is full of educated derelicts. Persistence and determination alone are omnipotent. The slogan "press-on" has solved, and always will solve, the problems of the human race"

Calvin Coolidge

"Never, never, never give up"
> *Winston Churchill*

"It is not so much brilliance as effort that is appreciated here as to determination to accomplish something"
> *FDR - editorial to the freshman class at Harvard 1903*

"A pint of sweat will save a gallon of blood"
> *Gen. George S. Patton*

The goal of this chapter (and all the Pillar chapters) is to:

- Clarify what Perseverance is and what it is not.
- Underscore the central role that perseverance plays in innovation.
- Share what the experts say about perseverance.
- Introduce a mental model for perseverance

According to Webster:

PERSEVERE (v): to persist in a state, enterprise, or undertaking in spite of counter influences, opposition, or discouragement.

Of course, the word perseverance is a verb. An "action word" as my third grade teacher, Mrs. Williams, taught me. Perseverance is something that you _do_ and it is hard. Really hard.

In some cases a person can help define a certain trait. In the case of perseverance, Thomas Edison would serve as a great example. Edison Biographer, Bob Frost, wrote that, "he stands today as the most prolific inventor of history and the most creative force in the annals of business". Wow, that's quite a statement. Think about that – "the most creative force in the annals of business". So what exactly did he do again? It's amazing actually. This man invented, among other things, the light bulb and the system to power it, the telephone, the phonograph, the microphone, the hearing aid, the alkaline battery, and on and on and on. Thomas Edison owned or co-owned an *astounding* 1,093 patents!

Think of the industries that are founded on what he discovered and then made practical. Think of Thomas Edison the next time there is a power failure in your neighborhood and you will really be impressed.

Some would argue though that his greatest contributions were the way that he was able to harness knowledge, categorize it and use it. This is what his New Jersey Menlo Park laboratory was famous for. Others have written that his greatest contribution was the creation of a "systems approach" to invention itself. Indeed, virtually all technological breakthroughs are based on a systems approach. In other words, Edison invented more than just the light bulb he invented the system that allowed the invention to work – the conductors, couplings, switches, sockets, fuses, etc.

Was Thomas Edison an innovator? Absolutely. Did his inventions have commercial value? Unquestionably. Was Thomas Edison a genius? Of course he was. And you all know what he had to say about his own genius, **"Genius is 1% inspiration and 99% perspiration".** This is one of the most highly quoted sayings of all time.

There is another quote though that may have influenced his own. In fact, this quote hung on every wall of his Menlo Park lab, "There is no expedient to which a man will not resort to avoid the real labor of thinking" – Sir Joshua Reynolds. It sounds like Sir Joshua would have been in agreement with Mark Twain.

So what was the single strongest attribute of the man who brought the world the incandescent light, the telephone, and the phonograph? It was likely perseverance. This man had perseverance.

Consider the following:

- He tried over 800 different materials before finding one – tungsten – that could light his incandescent bulb without being consumed by it.
- When he announced that he was working on a machine that could talk, a prominent Yale professor commented that the idea of a "phonograph" was ridiculous. A French Scientist said that Edison's invention was a trick using a ventriloquist.

- He was obsessed with tinkering. So much so, that when he worked for a telegraph company, his co-workers called him "The loony".
- When Edison published his work on subdividing electrical current (so a system of bulbs could work if one burned out), the "experts" said these challenges couldn't be solved. A committee of the British government stated officially that commercial subdivision was "impossible".

Turn back to the dictionary definition for perseverance. Does this not describe Edison? It does. And that's one reason why perseverance, and true innovation, is so uncommon – because of the 99% perspiration part. The human condition would rather watch TV than persevere in pursuit of a goal laden with obstacles. We live in a world of instant gratification and sound bites. But as human beings we also delight in the stories of those who have succeeded against all odds and those who persevered and achieved something fantastic.

Unfortunately for Edison's family though, he did more than persevere throughout the course of his experiments, he was absolutely obsessed by his work. His work *was* his life. He could not separate who he was from what he did. As a result, his wives and children suffered from neglect.

MENTAL MODELS

A mental model has been created for each of the four pillars of innovation. A mental model is simply a graphic snapshot that will help you remember, and act upon, the key behaviors associated with each pillar.

The Inspiration/Perspiration Balance

The mental model for perseverance is a weight balance. On one of the balance trays there is a sweat drop. This represents the *perspiration*. On the other there is a light bulb – that's the *inspiration*. Maybe you will remember Edison when you look at the model. What's also evident in the model is that the tray with the sweat drop on it is much heavier than the side with the light bulb. This is as it should be since the balance we need to keep is very heavily weighted to the perspiration side. You and your team or your company, can use this as a quick visual check to see how you are doing. Mental models also have a few quick thoughts attached to them to stimulate some additional thinking.

- How is your I/P balance?
- Corporate Antibodies got you down?
- How can your management help you persevere?

Perseverance is not exactly the same as hard work. There is a subtle difference that we should explore. Hard work and perseverance are cousins, but they are not the same. The difference between the two is that perseverance recognizes a certain degree of risk and vision. In other words, with perseverance, there is no guarantee that all your hard work will ever pay out. People who persevere seem to be driven by a vision of something that pushes them beyond that which is completely rational. This was the case with virtually all the great inventions. The inventor, almost always "saw" something that no one else could – and believed in it. On the contrary, the rational man can describe, using perfect logic and examples, why something <u>can't work</u>. I have this quote on my desk that seems to sum up the rational man.

> *"The practical man adapts himself to the changing world. The irrational man attempts to change the world to suit himself. Therefore, all progress is made by irrational men".*
>
> *George Bernard Shaw*

Sadly, there are countless millions of rational men. Those that simply count the hours they work and the $/per hour that they get paid for their labor. This might be one equation for success, or a definition of "how life is", but it also sells the genius within all of us quite short.

Here is another thought on the difference between hard work and perseverance, this time from my first supervisor. We called them bosses back then not supervisors. Bernie Payne was wonderful. Having a Junior College degree, Bernie was not highly educated by corporate managerial standards. He was however smarter than virtually all of the high-powered MBAs who worked in the company at that time. Bernie was "country". He was always deeply tanned, slow of speech, but very quick of mind. It seemed that regardless of the situation, Bernie had already been there before. He consistently knew what people were going to do and say before they acted. He was amazing – and successful – at work, at home and in his second business. When everybody was running around like chickens with their heads cut off, Bernie would have a twinkle in his eye. Not only was he calm, he was amused by it all.

One day I was in his office explaining how hard I was working when he interrupted and asked me a question that I will always remember, "Jim, do you know what happens to people who work hard?" Of course I did! I babbled something incoherent about having a better chance of succeeding. Bernie simply replied, "They get tired". Then he grinned.

Wow, I really had to think about that one. I mean hard work had been pounded into my head since I was in infant. What Bernie was telling me though was that hard work, in and of itself, gets you <u>nothing</u>. No, you need to be really smart about how you are going to apply your energy - and against what you choose to persevere.

Perseverance and Courage

Perseverance has a close cousin as well. It's called courage. Courage, of course, is not about the absence of fear. Courage is about going forward in the face of fear. Consider again the illustration given earlier in the book about Henry Ford. It can be argued that he exercised considerable courage as he pursued his dream of the assembly line. In a similar way Swede Momsen also summoned up large degrees of courage as he fought the navy establishment in pursuit of his life-saving inventions. Courage and perseverance often go hand in hand.

What did Swede Momsen choose to persevere against? What did Edison? How about you?

PERSEVERANCE IS A VIRTUE – ENJOY IT!

Have fun with what you choose to persevere against. In many cases we were taught this as children. One of my favorite books was The Little Engine That Could. This book isn't about the virtue of hard work; it's about *believing* that you can do something. Another great business book, cleverly disguised as a children's book, is Oh the Places You'll Go by Dr Seuss. If you are in business this is a must read. This is all about "going on" in a scary and uncertain world, but having faith and courage during the journey. Read this to your kids or read this to your team.

As adults we absolutely love entertainment that features extreme perseverance. Consider these movie classics: The Incredible Journey, An Officer and a Gentleman, Hoosiers, Saving Private Ryan, and the greatest "guy-movie" ever made, RUDY. Don't we also love it when our favorite sports team perseveres and wins the championship? Nothing is sweeter.

Think of the achievements that you are most proud of in your life and reflect upon how you had to persevere to accomplish them. Remember what Emerson said, "No great thing was ever achieved without enthusiasm".

Speaking from 25 years worth of experience, I can't underscore the virtue of perseverance enough. To persevere is hard and it takes courage.

You have to persevere, when others don't believe in what you are doing including people in authority (including your own supervisor). As I look back at every major innovation that I have had a direct part in, I can say, without reservation, that there were naysayers. To be successful you have to overcome them. But one thing is for certain - you can expect them. Here is a small sampling.

Four years ago, I was directly involved with an innovation that now nets the company over $10MM annually. Revenues from this innovation are also growing at a 20% rate and the profit margin is better than the corporate average. Not too shabby. At the time however only a hand full of people believed that this idea had any chance of working. To help bolster awareness of the concept a "display" was set up in the lobby of the company in our corporate headquarters. This way everyone would have the chance to see the vision that my team was seeing. Here's what happened.

- The majority of the people walked right on by without even noticing.
- A few offered some kind words, but looked around to make sure nobody overheard them.
- One person, who was a Group Director of Marketing at the time, commented in a very discouraging tone, "Well, it's different".
- Another senior person took me aside and politely explained to me why the idea could never work!

What I learned is that the vast majority of people will not see your vision until it is up and running. And even then, expect it to take awhile. This same phenomenon occurred, in some fashion or another, with every major innovation that myself, or one of my teams, has ever been involved with.

Don't be discouraged by this. EXPECT THIS. This is human nature. Swede Momsen had skeptics, as did Edison, as did Henry Ford, as will you. To innovate, you and your team must overcome them through perseverance. This is not optional and it takes courage.

Hurdles to Overcome

There are basically two hurdles that you will encounter on your way to perseverance.

HURDLE #1 - OTHERS

"Others" can be boiled down to one word – politics. Politics can range from downright ugly to just plain silly. Innovators will feel politics simply because they are 1) ahead of everyone else 2) they are seeing things that others haven't imagined and 3) they are actually creating things that others haven't thought of. This naturally makes those that haven't thought of them first get defensive, a bit paranoid or otherwise "sideways" as follows. The following comments from others are typical:

- "Hey, did you hear what that new team is doing?"
- "That's our turf"
- "They aren't being good team players"
- "Who authorized them to do that?"

Remember what the Admiral said to Swede Momsen after his successful demonstration of the artificial lung? "Young man, what the hell have you been up to?" And remember the response he received from the Bureau of Naval Construction and Repair when he pleaded his case for the very devices that would save men's lives? That response was anything but receptive.

- Who the hell was this new lieutenant?
- Already two days on the job and he is pushing some screwball idea to get people out of submarines.
- His idea to boot!
- You'd think he was the first person to ever think of that problem. Well the bureau had been fooling around with it for years.

Here's the punch line though, exactly the same thing is happening in your company - or church or family. Guaranteed! Just insert any of the following for the Bureau of Navy Construction and Repairs and you'll have the same result: Research Department, Human Resources Department, Fund Raising Committee or Sales Force. This is a certainty. Bet the farm.

You have to persevere and fight back to become a successful innovator. It is important to remember though that corporate antibodies are people, even the worst of them. They are not evil. They do however see the world differently from the way you do. Remember, nobody sees the world as it is. They only see it from their own perspective. Almost always, however, corporate antibodies see a narrower view of the world, one that is based on a limited range of experiences. These people are sometimes driven by fear or the insecurity that manifests itself in the need to maintain the status quo – or control.

The corporate antibodies may never be on your Christmas card list but that's O.K. They may never be your best friends. That's not the goal. Sometimes, if you can get these people to "neutral" that is a victory. It's also a much more mature way of looking at it. Name-calling won't help and will always make things worse. Be patient, and persistent, and always remember that people will forget what you tell them but they NEVER forget how you made them feel.

HURDLE #2 - YOURSELF

To become a successful innovator, you have to overcome yourself. This may sound harsh but it isn't meant to be. Consider that we've reviewed the 99% perspiration part in detail, but we haven't given much ink to the 1% inspiration. Without it, there is no vision against which to persevere. But where does this spark come from? It comes from you. The spark is also easily snuffed out.

When I was a kid I loved the Boy Scouts. The Boy Scouts were made for Jim Marstiller. Camping, canoeing, hiking, Jamborees, etc, I loved the whole thing. The Jamborees, or gatherings of scouts from a wide area, were especially fun. They were meant to test your scout skills and involved friendly competition. These competitions consisted of a series of Boy Scout skill-games. One that clearly comes to mind was the competition to start a fire without matches. You had two minutes to do this. If you had a visible flame within two minutes you got 100 points for your patrol. No flame, no points. To make this plausible for 12-year-old boys, we were allowed to use flint and steel (to make a spark) and something called "charred cloth". Charred cloth was basically Dad's old T-shirt that had been burned to the point of blackening, but without actually being consumed by a flame. A poor man's charcoal if you will. Long story short, if a spark from your flint and steel hit the charred cloth, it had a reasonable chance of being nurtured into a flame. We would carefully build our fire using dry, small pieces of wood, with charred cloth at the base. When the judge said, GO, we would furiously strike the flint with the steel to try to get sparks to fly on the charred cloth. We would then *gently* blow on the cloth, get it to glow, and finally combust into a flame. When we accomplished this, and as I recall - only about 1/3 of the patrols could - it was a great feeling of accomplishment. Like a minor miracle – making fire without matches.. Pretty cool as I remember.

There are two fundamental lessons here. 1) You can't make a fire without a spark and 2) If you don't nurture that spark, it will go out for sure!

The sparks of innovation come from deep within each of us and for a variety of reasons. It's up to us to pay attention to that spark of an idea and to keep the spark going. The origin of sparks, and nurturing of them, will be reviewed in much more detail in <u>Chapter 5 - Knowledge</u>.

Tips on Overcoming Others and Yourself to Persevere

- Avoid spark-killers and psychic vampires as they can suck the enthusiasm out of any situation including life itself.
- Don't get angry with corporate antibodies – at least publicly. Stay focused and cheerful instead. Let your light shine and play your game.
- Be an energy-giver – not an energy-taker.
- Don't take things personally when your ideas are criticized, even when the criticisms seem aimed at you. Rise above it!
- Remember that you are not alone. Every great innovator went through what you are faced with.

- Have a buddy that shares your vision. Make disciples. Spread the word
- Have courage – the first cousin of perseverance.
- Have fun. Remember, you are not trapped in a submarine on the bottom of the ocean. You are more likely working for a company that makes widgets or sells something. So don't take yourself too seriously. It will sap your energy if you do. Remember, the Cat in the Hat had it all figured out when he said, "It's fun to have fun, but you've got to know how"
- Finally, remember that what you do and what you are, are two different things.

Conversations with Dr. Fickeler

I came to the conclusion early on that the perspective of an expert in human behavior would be helpful in understanding the drivers of innovation. As a result, I sought out someone to assist me who was intelligent, experienced, highly educated, and had an abundance of common sense. That search led me to Dr. Jennifer Joerding Fickeler. Jennifer is a consultant in the field of psychology specializing in understanding the behavior of individuals and organizations. Specifically her experience includes organizational measures, employee, customer and consumer satisfaction, managing change and training. Her current emphasis is on team dynamics and development, information sharing, and innovation. Not only is Jennifer highly qualified she also has the ability to communicate the intricacies of human behavior to me in plain English.

In this chapter on perseverance, and the three additional "pillar chapters" that follow, brief recaps of my conversations with Dr. Fickeler will be included. These summaries will allow you to benefit from her insights and that of other experts in the field that she has researched.

To follow is a brief summary of our conversations on perseverance as a pillar of innovation.

- The leading innovation researchers agree that perseverance is crucial to the innovation process. They further make the distinction that while perseverance is an innovation virtue; it tends to reflect two personality types.

- The first type reflects someone who has made up their mind in advance that they will persevere to the end – no matter what. In a sense, this first type pursues the innovation with a dogged determination. They will pursue the goal until it is no longer possible to attain it. The second type reflects someone whose perseverance is linked more to a pre-meditated process. These people will map out the steps along the way and will continue, or persevere; as long as the work still makes sense after each step (i.e. they keep checking the feasibility and desirability of achieving the goal). These people pursue perseverance "with an awareness" and likely have a higher success ratio in innovating. It is interesting to note though that neither type is necessarily "better" than the other. The reality is that organizations need both personality types as they strive to innovate.

- There is also a direct correlation between the ability of individuals to persevere and their level of self-esteem. More specifically, people with high self-esteem have higher expectations for themselves and don't want to quit. These same people will also persist longer if new alternatives become available to them throughout the innovation process. These people tend to be more flexible in their ability to consider alternative routes that could lead to their innovation goal.

Chapter 4 Key Learning

1. Perseverance is not synonymous with hard work and is not always rational
2. Perseverance is a central ingredient in innovations and success stories
3. Success stories that do not include perseverance are called "lucky".
4. Perseverance is a personal choice. And it takes courage.
5. Perseverance is linked to an individual's self-esteem.

Self-help for Persevering:
Your 90-Day Prescription

1. It is a fact that nothing of lasting value was ever accomplished without hard work. However, sometimes the prospect of persevering through a tough situation can seem like a sacrifice that's too large. I know that is the case in my own life as well because I'm a common person maybe a lot like you. To be honest, if I would have known up-front how much work certain endeavors were going to take (like writing this book), I might not have had the will to persevere.

New Perspective to be gained: Don't think of perseverance as sacrifice, think of perseverance as a wonderful act of self-indulgence. By persevering you are making an incredible investment in yourself. As a result, you will be much better prepared to handle all the future challenges in life. Every time you persevere and accomplish something of lasting value, all the hurdles that you will face FOR THE REST OF YOUR LIFE will be easier to get over. Persevere BECAUSE you want a wonderful and fulfilling life.

2. Exercise to Perform: Think of all the times in your life that you have persevered through difficult circumstances and write them down. Think of all the times that you have achieved something of lasting value. Perhaps you persevered to win a science fair project, you became an Eagle Scout, won a high school athletic letter, won academic recognition, won a band competition, won a championship, won a meaningful award at work, graduated from college, or made it through basic training in the military. Now ask yourself this question, "If I would have known up-front how much work these endeavors were going to take, would I still have done it"? The answer to that question might be NO but that's O.K. We were not designed to know the future. If we were, we would be overcome with anxiety. Instead, celebrate what you have accomplished and reflect on how that has enabled you to grow. The rest of your life will be more meaningful and easier if you do.

3. Lifestyle Change to Make: Become committed to making a difference in the social structure of your community. Specifically, join an organization that volunteers its time and talents to making things better. If there is a major annual event, perhaps a fundraiser or a membership drive, jump in and make a difference. If this event requires a lot of hard work and perseverance to be successful, then that's even better. This is a wonderful way to quickly see the positive outcomes that result from perseverance. You will feel great about what you have accomplished. You will also build a wonderful network with other people committed to persevering and you will see how your efforts are helping others.

4. **Book to read**: *The Terrible Hours* by Peter Mass

5. **Movie to Watch**: **Rudy.** Average High School football player overcomes impossible odds to play for Notre Dame. Rudy becomes the only player in modern day Notre Dame History to be carried off the field after a victory. Perhaps the ultimate motivational movie (or at least, guy motivational movie).

Chapter Five – Knowledge

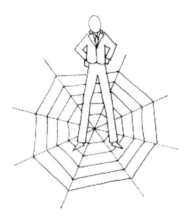

"If history teaches us anything it is that man, in his quest for knowledge and progress, is determined and cannot be deterred"

and

"In a time of turbulence and change, it is more true than ever that knowledge is power"

John F. Kennedy

"When you know a thing, to hold that you know it: and when you do not know a thing, to allow that you do not know it – this is knowledge"

Confucius

"All men by nature desire knowledge"

Aristotle

"The whole of science is nothing more than a refinement of everyday thinking"

Albert Einstein

"Knowledge is Good"

Inscription on the statue from the opening scene in *Animal House*.

According to JFK, Confucius, Aristotle, Albert Einstein and the likes of John Belushi; knowledge:

- Cannot be deterred and is linked to perseverance
- Is power
- Is desirable
- Is embedded in what you know - and what you know you *don't* know
- Is similar to common sense and
- Is good

That's quite an eclectic gathering of related thoughts. What does it all boil down to and how does it specifically relate to the process of innovation?

Of the four pillars of innovation, it is arguable that KNOWLEDGE is the most intriguing. It is also the pillar that people feel the need to put an asterisk next to.

There was universal agreement among the experts that were interviewed for this book that Perseverance, Risk and Passion are central to the innovation process. Specifically, the following words were commonly used to describe their relevancy:

- Imperative
- Critical
- Absolute
- Extremely important
- Fundamental

When it came to KNOWLEDGE though, key distinctions had to be made. Specifically, KNOWLEDGE, while central to the innovation process, is unique in that it doesn't have to be possessed by one person. Not all the knowledge has to reside in one person's head. Certainly, knowledge is acquired from your own experiences, but it is also acquired, and accelerated, through your association with others. An individual can have great knowledge in one or more areas, but to be highly innovative, that person must *also:*

1) Seek and value the knowledge from others in related fields and
2) Develop the ability to "connect the dots".

Knowledge in isolation is not enough. Magic is created when individual knowledge is combined with the knowledge of others. This is when true breakthrough occurs.

According to Webster's, KNOWLEDGE is defined as follows:

KNOWLDEGE (n) (1) the fact or condition of knowing something with familiarity gained through experience or association and (2) the range of one's information or understanding.

Webster's definition actually does a wonderful job of outlining the essence of how knowledge is key to the innovation process. We will review each part of the definition in more detail.

The first part of the definition talks in terms of gaining familiarity through experience <u>or</u> association. This is a key for better understanding how innovation works.

1. Gaining Knowledge through Experience

• **Knowing something through <u>experience</u>.** This relates to the personal experiences that we've had – i.e. those experiences that we've had in our lives and our careers. Like most things in life, it also boils down to <u>quality</u> learning experiences that have led to gaining new perspectives and wisdom. What are some of those experiences that have truly generated new perspectives? They can be categorized into three buckets.

1. <u>Education:</u> In this reference, we are talking about formal education. With certainty, your education has a big influence on how you see the world as your education usually reflects your aptitude. My brother is an engineer and I am a businessman. Same parents, but with totally different educations and aptitudes.

2. <u>Career Experiences:</u> Career experiences have a major influence on your perspective of the workplace. If your career has been in finance, you will see the world much differently from someone who has had a career in sales.

3. <u>Real-life</u>: Forget education and career for a minute. Think about the perspective-altering experiences that you have had in real life. Can anything be more powerful than those? Those perspectives gained through:
   • Having a baby
   • Growing up in poverty (or abundance)
   • Growing up in an dysfunctional home
   • Being in the military
   • Being a coach
   • Being an elected official
   • Playing an instrument
   • Being a minority
   • Serving on a charitable board
   • Being a parent
   • Having global experience
   • Being on a championship team
   • Having a "handicap"
   • Being a CEO

- Being a woman (or a man)
- Being in love

In all these cases the perspective cannot be gained unless you have "been there". Period. In other words, there is no substitute for experience and experience is one of the keys to accumulating knowledge. Each of these categories of experience: education, career, and real life, make up your base of relevant knowledge.

It is accepted as a truism that "you can't lead from experiences that you haven't had". In a similar fashion, you cannot innovate from a base of knowledge that you don't possess. Your knowledge however is much more than the sum of experiences that you have accumulated. It is also about the quality or intensity of the experience.

In Education: Quality in education is self-evident. Someone with a degree in engineering from the University of Michigan, for example, has a deeper base of knowledge in his field than someone with an Associate's degree in engineering from a Community College. And the person with the associate's degree has a much deeper understanding of engineering than does the High School student who is a good math student.

In Your Career: Career experiences enhance formal education. It's one thing to understand the academics. Book learning is important. Often it's the "foot" that gets you in the door. However, it is the quality in your career experience that reflects what the marketplace is willing to pay. An engineer with 20 years experience with Lockheed Aerospace, or with Microsoft, will command a greater salary than, a) an engineer with 5 years of experience at those same companies or b) an engineer with 20 years at companies with a lesser reputation.

In your Life: Quality comes into play here too of course. Someone who spent four years in the Navy for example does not have the same depth, or intensity, of experience as someone who was also a Navy Seal. And the Navy Seal will not experience the same intensity of experience as the serviceman who has also faced combat.

No doubt, quantity and quality are key ingredients that add to your knowledge base. One way of looking at them might be like understanding how to ride a bike.

- Formal education might involve watching videos on bike riding, reading books about bike races, and studying the mechanics of how the gears add leverage to your pedaling power.
- Career and real life will include the experiences associated with actually riding bikes – riding different kinds of bikes, racing bikes, riding under different conditions, in different countries, etc.

It is the summation of these relevant experiences – quality and intensity - that allows us to accumulate part of the knowledge we need to innovate.

Gaining Knowledge through Cross-Functional Experience

Cross-functional experience is tremendously important and highly relevant to the innovation process. Cross-functional knowledge is borne from having multiple quality experiences. The smart companies aggressively support cross-functionality in the workplace. They support cross-functional career-pathing and reward those that have gained multiple perspectives through these experiences. It is becoming increasingly common that CEOs, for example, have had multiple experiences throughout their career. It is also self-evident that employees that possess multiple quality experiences will be able to view the world from a broader perspective.

An individual's ability to innovate, or facilitate the innovation process, is <u>exponentially proportionate</u> to the cross-functional experiences he or she has had.

Examples:

- In <u>education</u>: The person with degrees in Business ***and*** Engineering (or Accounting *and* Law, etc)
- In <u>career:</u> The person who has successfully a) managed data *and* people or b) who has successfully led accountants *and* salespeople, etc.

- <u>In life</u>: The person who is a father <u>*and*</u> coach (or mother <u>*and*</u> board member, etc, etc)

2. Gaining Knowledge through Association

Reviewing Webster's definition again - KNOWLDEGE (n) (1) the fact or condition of knowing something with familiarity gained through experience ***or association***. (2) the range of one's information or understanding.

When it comes to knowing something with familiarity gained through experience or association, PERSPECTIVE is the key. Here's what two great minds have to say about perspective.

Stephen Covey said, "Nobody sees the world as it is, they only see it through their own perspective".

Abraham Maslow, father of the famous "Man's Hierarchy of Needs" model, said, "He who is good with a hammer sees every problem as a nail".

The learning is this – a limited perspective, or set of tools, rarely leads to knowledge sufficient to deliver a meaningful solution.

KNOWLEDGE is like an elephant. While standing close to an elephant you cannot see the whole thing. One person will be looking at its ears, another at its tusks, and yet a third at its tail. They are all looking at the same elephant, at the same time. Yet they will all be seeing and describing something quite different. Worse yet, they will all be convinced that what they are seeing represents the truth about elephants. To them, what others are seeing, or their opinion, just isn't right. There will be issues relating to trust. After all, how can you trust someone who describes an elephant in terms of its ears, when your frame of reference is tusks? The man looking at the tail is equally convinced of what he sees. He is an expert in tails. When someone asks him to describe an elephant he describes the tail. His area of expertise, experience, and of education – is tails. "I know what I see". I know what I'm doing. I'm a professional (and you are not!) will be the inference!

The more perspectives you have of the elephant, the more likely you are to understand what an elephant really is.

Here is the punch line: we all think we see the whole elephant. In reality though, we only see part of it. We are standing much closer to the elephant than we think. This is true of individuals, teams and entire organizations. People, teams and organizations that think they see the whole elephant are either 1) mistaken 2) arrogant, or 3) not innovative.

The only way to see the whole elephant is to openly seek, and listen to, people that see the elephant from a different vantage point. Examples include:

- Trainers
- Groomers
- Zoo keepers
- Big Game hunters
- The native people who live near elephants
- Veterinarians
- Historians
- Wildlife Artists

These different people all contribute to a more complete understanding of what an elephant really is. Become partners with these people. Spend a lot of time with them. They have a very similar passion as you do and they love to talk. Listen to them. To see the whole elephant you also have to get dirty. Pick up a shovel! If you do, you will be infinitely better equipped to develop something of commercial value as it relates to elephants.

3.   Gaining Knowledge through a Range of Information or Understanding

Association is also crucial because it leads directly to the last part of Webster's definition. Specifically, "the <u>range</u> of one's information or understanding" defines knowledge. Associated knowledge allows you to have more range. This is key. It is also fairly simple. Associated knowledge is crucial because it allows you to have more "dots to connect". We've all heard about the skill of connecting the dots. Some people seem to have a wonderful ability to connect things. They seem to have an uncanny ability to take two or more separate pieces of information and connect them in such a way as to create something new and different. Connecting these dots is a skill that innovators possess.

Do innovators have some sort of 6th sense that the rest of us don't have? Absolutely not, but they do posses **more dots**. The innovator has many more potential dots, or relevant experiences, to connect than the average person (e.g. all the different elephant roles listed previously represent different dots). Everything else being equal, the one with the most dots to connect has the best odds of connecting things in new ways. They have stacked the odds in their favor, just like the trophy fisherman in chapter 1.

The Web of Knowledge

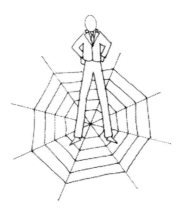

81

Our mental model for knowledge is a spider web. This is because the ability, or potential, to innovate is analogous to a web. The larger the web, the better the odds of the spider catching dinner. And the larger your personal web of knowledge, the better the odds of you successfully innovating. The key questions therefore become:

- How big is your web of knowledge?
- Are there holes in your personal web?
- How about your team, or your company's, web?

CONSIDER THE FOLLOWING WEBS

1) <u>Very limited</u> – This one has only a few rings and spokes. It is a web full of holes. We'll call this one "Joe's web". His web consists of a Bachelor's degree in Zoology, but with no experience and virtually no outside contacts.
2) <u>Medium web</u> – This one has a moderate number of rings and spokes. We'll call this one "Mary's web". She has the same degree as Joe <u>but</u> with 10 years experience (in 3 different companies) and with a fair number of contacts in her field.
3) <u>Large web</u> – This one has dozens of rings and spokes and only small holes. We'll call this one Diane's web. She has the same experience as Joe and Mary but has additional experiences as follows: A Master's Degree in Environmental Science, 20 years experience (with 5 different companies on 3 different continents), is multi-lingual, has won amateur competitions in wild-life photography, and knows hundreds of people in the field.

Key Learning:

1. Trying to innovate with a web that is too small is like looking for a lost item in the wrong place. You keep looking and looking but you can't find it. One of three results is sure to follow:

- Frustration
- The conclusion that it cannot be found or
- The conclusion that "there's nothing more that can be invented here"

The innovator knows better. She knows that you're just looking in the wrong place! Build a bigger web.

2. Most people's webs are smaller than they think. Like standing too close to the elephant, we think we see the elephant. Upon further review, most people/teams/companies will realize that their webs are either too small, have big holes in them or both.

3. Spiders are master engineers who are both innovative and creative. Did you know that no two webs are exactly alike? Spiders also:

- o Have PASSION – If the spider doesn't catch something, it will starve. They are motivated!
- o Have KNOWLEDGE – They know how to build their webs.
- o Accept RISK – They have to sit on their web where a predator (e.g. a bird, wasp or person) can get them if they want to catch something themselves.
- o Have PERSEVERANCE – A spider will remain motionless on his web for hours just waiting, and *knowing*, that the payoff is on its way.

Beyond Elephants and Spiders

I am convinced that my own ability to innovate is directly related to my many experiences. I've had the good fortune of building a very large personal web. I didn't start out to build a big web, but it happened. My web expanded and got filled in over the years and yours will too. My personal web is made of the following rings and spokes.

Formal Education:

- • Bachelor of Science – Emphasis in Microbiology
- • Master of Science – Food Science
- • Master of Business Administration (MBA) – Marketing emphasis

The academic disciplines of science and business are very different. Most importantly, they allow you to fundamentally think differently and to understand different perspectives.

<u>Career Experiences</u>:

- Product Research and Development: (3 different companies – 2 very different industries)
- Marketing - Brand Management: (multiple categories of consumer packaged goods)
- Sales: Line and Staff – HQ and field
- Consulting – domestic and international
- Vice President and Managing Director in a top-50 worldwide company
- Global Director in a business development role.
- I have over 1,200 contacts on my PDA. These equate to many, many different (and valuable) perspectives.

When you are described as experienced, that means that you have made a multitude of mistakes and hopefully learned from them. Having made mistakes and being experienced go hand in hand. Mistake making will be discussed in more detail in the chapter on risk.

<u>Some Personal Life Experiences</u>:

- Father, husband, coach, teacher, speaker , board member
- Observer of nature, wilderness explorer, fisherman, Eagle Scout
- Musician and athlete (nothing special on either account though!)
- Author, businessman and entrepreneur
- Christian

Quality life experiences are vital to your overall ability to build a quality web. So keep building! I find that the innovation process becomes easier as I accumulate more quality experiences. It will be the same with you. Seek quality life experiences and your ability to connect the dots and innovate will increase exponentially.

As was mentioned in the beginning of the book I received the Innovator of the Year Award in 2000 and 2001. Looking back on the circumstances that led up to the innovations, several things are readily apparent.

1. There was a wide range of associated knowledge that was put to use. In the example of the <u>Learning Center (mentioned in the beginning of the book – 2000 Award Winner)</u>, over 70 vendor partnerships were formed. Some were informal, involving nothing more than a non-disclosure agreement, and some were official Joint Ventures. The point is that our team developed a view of the elephant we couldn't have seen on our own. Dots were connected in new ways to create a new result.

2. The knowledge that was used to develop the Learning Center was <u>specific, not general</u>. There was a great depth of knowledge surrounding this particular subject area. The team had identified an elephant as the object of our innovation and not just any animal or even a pachyderm. Perspectives with no grounding in the particular area we were looking for were not sought. We had focus. Remember, when Swede Momsen invented his lifesaving devices, he was <u>an expert</u> in the area of various mixtures of gases: helium, oxygen and nitrogen. But he didn't gain this knowledge by himself. He had a whole team of medical doctors, deep-sea divers, and researchers. He connected the dots.

3. The knowledge was not all my own. And that's fine with me. I had a very good depth of understanding in the area we were exploring but my personal KNOWLEDGE was incomplete. You can't consistently innovate all by yourself.

Conversations with Dr. Fickeler

I found my conversations with Dr. Fickeler on the subject of knowledge both interesting and highly relevant. Knowledge sharing (i.e. web-building) is a topic that Jennifer is quite passionate about. So much so that it was the subject of her doctoral dissertation.

The bottom line is this – an organization's ability to identify and extract the <u>unique</u> experiences from its best people is integral with its ability to innovate. That is a pretty big statement. Taking this one step further, the health of the modern organization is directly related to getting people to share what they know with each other.

People are unique and have encountered very different experiences throughout life's journey. As a result, individuals possess very different domains of knowledge. By pooling this knowledge, organizations get smarter and more efficient in solving their problems. Again, the challenge becomes getting others to share information.

To facilitate this sharing, organizations are focusing on the power of the group. Talented teams are rapidly replacing talented individuals as the preferred path for generating consistent innovation. There are good reasons for doing this. The "collective IQ" of a team is greater than any one person, regardless of talent. Research shows that groups that have good sharing dynamics tend to be more self-confident and productive[7,8]. This is becoming increasingly self-evident and is the wave of the future.

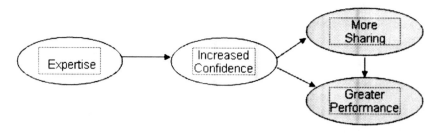

While this may be self-evident it is also not easy. How do you encourage good team play and get people to share their unique experiences and perspectives? Yet, this is integral to the formation of innovative ideas. It is in this sharing of the unique skills and talents that "the dots" are identified and later connected.

However, there are many pitfalls awaiting those looking to tap individual talent for the good of the team (and organization). There are several reasons why people are not willing to share (even when they have something relevant to say).

By nature, group dynamics involve a social setting. Where there is social setting, there is always the potential of social risk. Social risk involves the perception of not belonging. There can be a powerful negative stigma associated with not belonging to a certain group that individuals want to avoid. The drivers of this are often rooted in a company's culture. We will briefly examine three cultures that inhibit sharing:

- A consensus culture
- A hierarchical culture
- A no-risk culture

A consensus culture is one where there is a premium placed on agreeing with one another. In its extreme form, the importance of agreeing is actually placed ahead of the importance of driving the business. The "goal" of meetings in a heavily consensus-driven culture is to seek out that which we already know. From there it will be confirmed that this is what we know and therefore this is what is determined to be the "truth". Any thoughts which are shared that are not in line with what is already known are seen as rude. This is the result of a powerful social moray to comply and conform. This type of culture is often associated with the Japanese. The Japanese have a saying, which translates in English as "the nail that sticks out gets hit". The inference is clear – conform or get hit by a hammer. This doesn't exactly foster new thoughts. While this culture does exist in Japan it is also alive and well in some companies in the United States. Managers that want to drive innovation will recognize these destructive social habits and facilitate their dismantling.

A hierarchical culture is one where the people higher up the organizational chart are heavily deferred to in all matters relating to knowledge. While there is no substitute for experience, it just might be that the junior people have the best perspective on what needs to be done. They have fresh eyes and thoughts. They may have just joined from a new company or are just out of school. They are often more technologically astute. What they think is important might be quite relevant. I have seen extreme examples of hierarchical cultures where junior people are literally not allowed to speak in meetings. A logical thought would be; if the company didn't want to know what these people think, why were they hired in the first place? The rational answer is that the company put more value maintaining the hierarchy than considering divergent thought. To not tap into their thoughts is to not honor diversity. Smart managers and companies know diversity – diversity in thought experience, education, race, gender, age, etc – is a great strength to be leveraged.

A no-risk culture is where perceived risks are to be avoided at all costs. The key of course is in what is perceived as a risk. In these cultures, anything that is different from what has been done before is defined as a risk. In extreme cases, anything new is looked upon with skepticism because "that's not the way we have done things in the past". (Does this sound familiar?) People who are steeped in this thinking will point to anything to avoid that which is new. They will reference data, "expert opinion" and play on the fear of what might happen if something goes wrong. A culture of no-risk is a culture of fear. A culture of courage is what companies must exhibit to innovate. The best leaders will support courageous thinking.

Where there is a consensus, no-risk, <u>and</u> hierarchical culture, there will be a total lack in innovation.

Of course, the danger associated with all of these types of cultures is that they discourage knowledge sharing. In particular, they discourage the sharing of the unique knowledge which companies need most to innovate.

Chapter 5 Key Learning

1. Knowledge is an indispensable ingredient in innovation
2. Knowledge is derived from one's personal experiences including education, career and life.
3. A depth of knowledge in one particular field is key.
4. The ability to innovate is directly related to the number of dots (or quality experiences) that can be connected.
5. Knowledge bases can be both personal and associated.
6. Smart leaders will recognize cultures that retard innovation and take steps to change them.

Self-help for Knowledge:
Your 90-Day Prescription

1. **<u>Perspective to be gained</u>:** Knowledge is not the same as intelligence. Knowledge, within the context of driving innovation, is the process of gaining multiple experiences. These, in turn, lead to the creation of a network of knowledge contacts. This is good news as building an innovation network is something that is <u>your choice</u> to develop. Your raw intelligence quotient (i.e. I.Q) on the other hand is something you are born with. Research shows however that the ability to innovate is a skill that can be learned. Specifically, it shows that those with just slightly higher than average I.Qs, are just as likely to innovate as the so-called geniuses.

2. **<u>Exercise to Perform</u>:** Remember, the knowledge that drives innovation is based on fusing multiple perspectives through a network of varied experiences. Here are some ways to gain new perspectives: learn a new language (this might provide a chance to hone your perseverance skills too!), learn how to play a musical instrument, learn a new skill – computer, carpentry, painting, or research a topic that has always interested you. They will all expand your perspectives and knowledge base.

3. **<u>Lifestyle change to make</u>**: Read. Make reading an integral part of your life. Read at least one book a month. Consider joining a book club or start one yourself. Remember, that those who choose not to read are no better off than those who can't read. Reading is the best way to get into the minds of the most interesting and brilliant people who have ever lived. Reading is also economical. Reading is integral to growing our intellect. You can change without growing, but you cannot grow without changing. Read to grow. Where will you get the time to read? It's always a choice. Start with turning off the TV. Some of the busiest people I know are also voracious readers. There is nothing better to do on airlines either. Read, don't watch the movie!

4. **<u>Books To read</u>**: *Man's Search for Meaning* by Victor Frankel

5. **<u>Movie to Watch</u>**: *Amadeus*

Chapter Six – Risk

"Take calculated risks. That is quite different from being rash"
Gen. George S. Patton

"I have suffered the consequences associated with many calamities in my life, a few of which actually occurred"
Mark Twain

"The Pioneers take the arrows"

Unknown

"Life is a daring adventure or nothing at all"
                                        Helen Keller

Here is how Webster defines risk

RISK (n) 1: possibility of loss or injury. 2: a dangerous element or factor.

Well no wonder we avoid risk. According to Webster, the consequences associated with risk range from something mildly unpleasant to death depending on the circumstances!

This is how we are brought up. Our mothers tell us be careful. Our fathers lecture us on the dangers associated with risky business ventures. Risk is most readily associated with something bad.

Culturally we think of risk in terms of caution or prudence. Risks are to be avoided. The word risky has negative connotations. "It sounds like a wonderful opportunity, BUT it's a little risky", <u>not</u> "It sounds like a wonderful opportunity, <u>AND</u> it's a little risky".

As a culture, Americans in particular, are brought up to be cautious, conservative and to avoid risks. We are also brought up a little bit negative. Think for a moment about the road signs we see every day. We have stop lights. Those stoplights have green lights too. Why are they never referred to as "go" lights? We are warned "slow -curve ahead". Why don't we see signs that read, "Straightaway coming, start speeding up"? Instead of a sign that reads, "Slippery when wet" how about one that reads, "Great traction when dry – hit the gas!". You get the point.

What road signs do you have in your brain that are negative and are causing you to slow down?

I literally have a full size stop sign in my office. Instead of it being red with the word STOP on it, it is green with the word GO. People love that sign. They want to know where they can get one.

Defining RISK within the Context of Innovation.

The question becomes how <u>should we</u> think about risk? Maybe we need to redefine what risk is really about and how the use of the word is evolving. Certainly we are all familiar with the old expression "nothing ventured, nothing gained". That suggests that there is a positive side to risk- taking and that risk is a precursor to something gained. In the 21ˢᵗ century, people seem to be expressing a desire to redefine risk itself. Not only do I suggest is this healthy and good, this is <u>necessary</u>.

Taking this thought one step further it has recently become popular to say, "Sometimes, the greatest risk is not taking one". This saying is becoming so common in fact, that it was even the tagline in an advertising campaign for a financial management company.

That suggests quite a change of thinking in the general populace. Think about that for a moment. In the financial community, that bastion of conservatism, we are evolving from thinking about risk from "not moving" to "moving". In other words, your personal financial security may depend more on being flexible and catching the wind vs. seeing which way the wind blows. We are evolving from thinking of financial security in terms of "getting a piece of the rock" to "sometimes the greatest risk is not taking one".

A related notion is that we need to question is the nature of security itself. Historically you will find, particularly in Western cultures, that security is synonymous with being stationary. Traditionally that stability is associated with staying put or not moving (e.g. a piece of the rock). Let's review some of the so-called truisms regarding traditional security.

We will explore these and then uncover why this thinking is not only incorrect, but that it's dangerous and counterproductive to delivering innovation.

Some would argue that the keys to job security are to:

- Stay in one place
- Stay in one department
- Stay in one division
- Stay in one company
- Stay in one country
- Stay with one supervisor

Bottom line: Just "stay put". I have a mental picture of a person saying to their dog "stay". Just stay. Don't move. Don't change as moving = danger.

Additional common wisdom regarding security:

- Don't rock the boat
- Don't stand out – as in "the hammer hits the nail that stands out".
- Don't be controversial
- Don't go against the flow
- Don't speak up -or at least wait until the VP speaks to see which way the wind is blowing.

In other words it's better to straddle the fence than to fall off either side.

These points can be summarized in two words DON'T CHANGE. Don't change because change = risk, and risk = something bad could happen. Of course, those who offer up this type of advice are very well meaning. They are likely trying to help others. Almost universally these people have good intentions. It is also said that, "the streets in hell are lined with good intentions".

However, this line of common reasoning is all wrong. Mark Twain said, "I've found that common sense ain't so common". When you stop to think about it, it's obvious as to why. The *greatest* way to incur damage or pain is to become a target. And the best way to become a target that is easy to hit is to NOT MOVE. Said another way, if you don't want to get hit, don't become a stationary target. Keep moving. Don't become a sitting duck!

That's how it works in nature and this is how it works in our world as well. At a business meeting I attended some years ago, the following story was shared about the "lion and the gazelle".

"It is said that every day on the African plain a gazelle awakes and thinks, I must run faster than the fastest lion today or I won't see the sun set. At the same time a lion awakes on the African plain and thinks, I must run faster than the slowest gazelle today or I will grow weaker, starve and then die". Of course the moral of the story is that it pays to keep moving - and move really fast. This is nature's way. This is survival of the fittest. This is all about strengthening the gene pool and natural selection. This is common sense.

Now, consider this scenario. What if a different gazelle awoke that day and thought, "I'm scared, I don't want to get eaten today. I am going to lie down in the tall grass and hope that the lion never finds me" Not a real good strategy.

Perspective and attitude are the keys. Which gazelle has the greatest security, the one who awakes alert, is fit, and is ready to run, or the one that is cowering in the grass? We all know people who have attempted to manage their career (or someone else's) like the gazelle in the grass, and often with the best of intentions.

Now, think about a hypothetical *third* gazelle who might awake on that African plain and thinks, "I'm gonna kick some serious lion butt today!" That gazelle won't be around for long either. That is what Patton referred to when he said, "Take calculated risks. That is quite different from being rash". It pays to be the first gazelle.

The Frog in the Pot

Our mental model for understanding risk is "the frog in the pot".

Perhaps you have heard the old fable about the frog in the pot? Long story short, it goes like this: if you drop a frog in a pot of hot water it will jump back right out. Obviously! *HOWEVER*, if you place a frog in a pot of room temperature water on a stove and then very gradually turn up the heat, the frog will turn into cooked frog legs rather than jump out! Now for the record, I have never verified this experiment and don't recommend trying it at home. The mental model though is quite clear. As long as the environment changes *gradually*, no matter how terrible it is, the frog would rather cook than change. This is not only the nature of frogs; it is human nature as well.

Consider for a moment people who are in careers that they don't like. Maybe their career is beyond "don't like", it's gotten to the point of hate and contempt. They hate their careers and dread getting up in the morning to go to work, BUT they have been doing it for over 30 years! Why? They do this because of the uncertainty associated with change. In other words the perceived risk is greater than the certainty of their current condition. They are like the frog in the pot.

Further consider people who may live within a terrible marriage. Maybe you've known someone like this? Their marriage has deteriorated to the point where it's beyond miserable. Perhaps there is verbal abuse, physical abuse, sexual abuse, or even drugs involved. Yet, they won't get out. Like the frog in the pot, the "comfort" they perceive within their immediate environment was still greater than the fear, or "the risk", associated with getting out. You want to scream at them – get out! But these individuals, like the frog, are working with an old mental model when it comes to risk and the fear associated with it.

This same phenomenon occurs in business and in every organization. It occurs with all types of frogs too – large, medium or small, old or young, spotted or striped. It can also be particularly common in either older or larger companies. Sometimes the frog, the frog in the pot, gets to thinking that:

- It has seen it all
- It has felt it all before
- It's life in the pot is a birthright
- The changes in the pot really aren't occurring
- It actually controls the environment in the pot

Of course these are all symptoms of arrogance and denial, but the end result is the same; bad judgment leading to disaster. The key learning is that the frog will get cooked (or the venerable company smoked) if it doesn't respond quickly to change. This consequence is independent from the frog's attitude and the points above describe an attitude. What's crucial is the ability to perceive REALITY and then take action – before it's too late!

Application to Business

Staying in the pot is not a good response to changing circumstances. This is not an acceptable approach to managing risk. In fact we all know intellectually (and instinctively) that the opposite is actually true. Specifically, companies, organizations and individuals *must* take some risks if real progress is to be made. RISK is an indispensable ingredient in the innovation process. The opportunity cannot be seized if the risk isn't taken. It is interesting to note that the Chinese symbol, or word picture, for risk is "opportunity riding on a dangerous wind".

A case study in American business will be used to underscore the importance of reacting when the heat gets turned up. Our example for risk involves Wal*Mart. It is not about Wal*Mart, but rather the reaction to Wal*Mart. No doubt Sam Walton was one of the greatest innovators of all time. He created a revolutionary new business model that set the retailing world on its collective head.

The Walton's are by far the richest family in America$_8$. The Walton heirs have more money than Bill Gates and Warren Buffet combined (almost $100 billion as of January 2005). How did Sam Walton build his empire and amass his enormous fortune? Sam Walton exuded the four pillars of innovation as follows.

Perseverance: The trials and tribulations of the early days were truly heroic. Some of them were also quite humorous in retrospect but Sam Walton had a vision, and he stuck to it. Beginning with one store in Arkansas in the 60's, Wal*Mart has become the world's largest company today.

Knowledge: Sam Walton was a genius – with people, with finances and with business.. He knew the details and he knew the big picture. He was a genius at connecting the dots and he built an enormous personal web of relationships.

Risk: Personal, Social, and Financial – they were all there by the bushel basket. This handsome, popular, athletic, Phi Beta Kappa scholar was going to do what with his life? Get into the 5 and Dime business? Start his own company?

Passion: To say that Sam Walton had passion would be an enormous understatement. He had a great lust for life and that was reflected in everything he did. He was charismatic. He was not only greatly respected and admired by his employees; he was truly loved by them. He loved them as well and they knew it. After Sam Walton's death, the company's logo was changed from Wal-Mart to Wal*Mart (i.e. from a dash to a star in between the Wal and the Mart). The star is in remembrance of Sam Walton.

His success story will not be the main focus of this chapter though. You might ask - why not? Isn't the Wal*Mart success story the perfect example of successful risk taking? Well it is the great example and it would be fun and easy to do, but there are two reasons why it won't.

1. Chances are, you are already pretty familiar with the Wal*Mart story. We wanted the *The Power to Innovate* to be fresh and offer new perspectives.
2. We'll review Wal*Mart briefly and then talk about *another story* – a related story that is equally fascinating. That story is about the retailing industry's reaction to Wal*Mart and the lessons to be learned about risk-taking.

To set up that story, a very brief history of Wal*Mart will be prudent. Call it a refresher.

Like Wal*Mart or not, what has been created, and how it was created is astounding. Wal*Mart, the brainchild of one man, Sam Walton, is simply the greatest business success story of all time.

- Wal*Mart is the largest company in the world, with annual sales in excess of a quarter of a trillion dollars.
- Wal*Mart has over 1,500,000 employees.
- Wal*Mart has WEEKLY shopper traffic in the United States alone is in excess of 100 million people.
- Wal*Mart owns over 13 square miles of retail floor space.
- $1,000 invested in Wal*Mart stock in 1972 would be worth over $2 million today.
- The Walton family is the richest in America.
- The wealth of the Walton family exceeds the annual gross domestic production of Singapore.

Sam Walton's incredible wealth wasn't built on technology – telecommunications, microchips, software, biotech or nanotech. It wasn't built on aerospace, pharmaceuticals, or oil. No, Sam Walton's wealth was built on pantyhose and groceries. Pantyhose and groceries!!

There have been numerous books written about Sam and his life and countless articles. You've probably read or heard the snippets about how he:

- Never flaunted his wealth.
- Always had his hair cut at the same small town barbershop

- Drove an average pickup truck. It's in the Wal*Mart museum in Bentonville, Arkansas – scratches and all.
- Was a business genius, and in particular, a genius when it came to working with people.

What Sam Walton did was create a behemoth based on 1) a new business model and 2) an incredible culture. Each will be briefly reviewed. Then the retail industry's reaction to what Sam Walton created will be detailed - the real emphasis of this chapter.

The Wal*Mart Business Model

The Wal*Mart business model is different. Very different. Totally revolutionary in its time. It is based on the principle that a "fast nickel" is more profitable then a "slow dime". Walton would offer merchandise at lower prices and make less money on each item. However he would take more money to the bank because of the greater total volume sold. Instead of selling two items a week and making 50 cents profit on each ($1 total profit) like his competition was doing (and is *still doing*), Walton would sell four items a week and make 30 cents each ($1.20 profit). His competition thought he was nuts. He would surely go out of business offering his ridiculously low prices.

Of course the rest is history and Sam Walton was no fool. To the contrary, Sam was brilliant. One of the smartest things he ever did was marry Helen, who in addition to being the love of his life, was also the daughter of the town's banker. He followed up this decision by buying the bank of Bentonville, Arkansas in 1961. Two very good moves for sure. Not only did Sam Walton have the vision for a totally new business model, he had the financing.

Sam Walton Fostered an Incredible Culture

Sam Walton often said that the success of his company was its people. He meant it and he was right. The Wal*Mart culture is a large part of their success. He also said that Wal*Mart's associates were the company's secret weapon because their culture couldn't be captured in the financial statements.

The Wal*Mart culture is a very powerful competitive weapon. Every morning before a Wal*Mart opens, the store's employees do two things. First, they review yesterday's sales and how they can do better today (quite a technological systems feat in-and-of-itself). Secondly, they give a cheer. They give a cheer! Every morning, they gather and give a very enthusiastic cheer. "Give me a "W", give me an "A", give me an "L", etc - cheer! They do it at Sam's Club too. The apostrophe in Sam's Club is referred to as a "squiggly" in Wal*Mart lingo. Are you serious? Yes! And when they get to that apostrophe in Sam's, they do a squiggly , which is kind of like Chubby Checker doing the twist!

It gets better. This unique culture is transferable -not only from state to state and from geography to geography but from country to country. If you can believe this, they do the Wal*Mart cheer in Germany. In Germany of all places! In fact, they did it so enthusiastically early one morning at a new store that the surprised neighbors called the police. If they build Sam's clubs in Germany, the Germans might be doing "squigglys" - a sure sign of the apocalypse!

Sam Walton was brilliant when it came to working with people. He treated everyone the same and he never forgot his roots. He was charismatic, enthusiastic, and humble. He was always willing to give all the credit to anyone who had a good idea. He visited his own stores constantly and built up an incredible repartee with his associates. They would run through a wall for "Mr. Sam". After all, here was a guy who was a billionaire and who drove a very ordinary pick-up truck, wore ordinary clothes and went hunting for birds and rabbits on the weekends. This was a person to whom they could relate.

The bottom line is this; he never put himself on a pedestal, he treated everyone the same and his employees absolutely loved him. The most amazing thing is, more than a decade after his death, they still do.

Here is my personal story that underscores that point. I was in a Sam's Club last year having new tires installed on my car. While I was waiting I bought some lunch – hot dog and a Coke. The price for a large juicy hot dog and a large Coke at Sam's? $1.55. Not bad. So I commented to the person behind the counter and told her how much I appreciated the low price of my lunch. Do you know how she responded to me? Did she say "thank you" or act indifferent or just plain act surprised? No, she smiled and said matter-of-factly, "Yes, Mr. Sam would be proud".

Business Model + Culture = Financial Success

Mr. Sam has also helped make a lot of people rich. Many, many Wal*Mart employees have become millionaires through the various profit-sharing plans; plans that were tied to the company's stock price. Not only was he sharing the credit, he was sharing the wealth.

I'll never forget my own experience in relation to this point. I was sitting in a small café in Fayetteville, Arkansas reading the local paper before heading to Bentonville for my Wal*Mart sales call. There was an article on the front page of the local paper detailing how an "ex-Wal*Mart store manager" had donated over $1 million to the University of Arkansas. Not an ex-Wal*Mart Senior Vice President, not an ex-Wal*Mart board member, or a family member - an ex-*store manager* had an extra million to give away. This was hardly an isolated incident.

The end result is that Wal*Mart has kicked some serious competitive butt for decades. And there is absolutely no end in sight. Consider for a minute.

- A new Wal*Mart or Sam's store opens someplace in America every 36 hours. Over 200 new stores every year.
- One of their largest problems now is keeping their own shelves stocked as shopper traffic continues to increase. At the rate of opening a new store almost every day, they can barely keep up with demand.
- Their compound annual <u>growth rates</u> are the envy of the industry. Of course, it's common knowledge that once you become enormous (e.g. General Motors, Exxon, IBM, etc) that you have to slow down. <u>Nobody told Wal*Mart</u>.
- Wal*Mart is the largest retailer outside the United States. This is even more amazing when you consider they have only been seriously operating internationally since the late 90's.

Will anything slow Wal*Mart's growth? Yes. There are several possibilities.

1. <u>Arrogance</u> – They could get cocky, become difficult to work with, and force their vendors into "lose-win" agreements. Despite what some would have you believe, this is not common practice. Having personally worked with the majority of top global retailers, including Wal*Mart, I have found them to be one of the best to work with. Historically, they have been tough but honest, and fair. Will this always be the case?

2. <u>Unionization</u> – The unions would love to get into Wal*Mart. This would cause Wal*Mart's labor costs to increase and impair their ability to further lower prices. All attempts to unionize have been thwarted to date. As long as Wal*Mart shares the wealth, it will be a "hard nut" for the unions to crack. A wild card in all this is Wal*Mart's stock price. This has a direct bearing on the compensation of their employees. In the past, whenever the stock is stagnant for more than 12-18 months, employees begin to grumble.

3. <u>Diminishing returns?</u> – Will Wal*Mart be able to maintain significantly lower prices indefinitely? At what point do they reach diminishing returns through supply chain and other efficiency investments? Wal*Mart's competitors will get smarter and smarter about how to address the everyday pricing gap.

4. <u>Government intervention</u> – Could the Government potentially break up Wal*Mart like Bell Telephone? Not likely. Break-ups are often predicated by evidence of consumers being short-changed through monopolistic practices. However, Wal*Mart's low-price practices are advantageous to shoppers.

5. <u>The Next Wal*Mart</u> – There eventually will be a new competitor that rises from nowhere to challenge, or at least frustrate, Wal*Mart. Is this new competitor Dollar General – the "hard discounter"? In many cases they have filled the vacuum left by Wal*Mart -in the small strip centers all over America that are now all but out of business. They are probably the fastest growing retailer that you never paid much attention to. They are also the answer to the following trivia question: "Which

American discount retailer has the fastest growth rate, the largest number of stores and also has high profit margins?"

6. <u>Next Generation?</u> Will the generations of Wal*Mart leaders that follow Sam Walton be able to maintain his legacy?

SO WHO'S THE FROG IN THE POT?

Perhaps the premier example of the frog in the pot is the American grocery business and its reaction, or lack of reaction, to Wal*Mart. For the most part, the grocery business has sat in the pot the last 15 years while Wal*Mart has turned up the heat. Only a few have jumped out. Many have been cooked. All are feeling the heat.

Question #1 – Who is the largest <u>grocer</u> in America (hint: <u>the largest by far</u> – by over $10 Billion in sales Vs second place)? Answer: Wal*Mart. Not Kroger. Not Safeway. Not Albertson's.

Question #2 – How many Wal*Mart stores sold groceries in 1990? Answer: 6. Not 106 or 600 – just 6. There are over 1,500 today.

If Sam Walton could say one thing to the American Grocery business from that big discount store in the sky it might just be this, *"Oh, it's not that warm in the pot. There is no need to change really; just keep doing what you are doing- everything will return to normal soon"*

While the Wal*Mart success is to be greatly respected, it is also directly linked to the inability of their competition to change.

In the Wake of Wal*Mart

It would be logical to associate the grocery industry with stability. After all, everybody has to eat. In a recession, food stocks are a logical refuge for our dollars. When everything else is unstable, there is stability in food. A safe haven if you will. There is a similar stream of logic in the beer business. People drink when times are good and they drink when times are bad. People like to drink.

When the economy is rocky, it would seem to make sense to invest in the food industry. This includes those who make it, ship it, warehouse it, and sell it. Perhaps the grocery industry is the very symbol of stability in a chaotic world.

There is also something all-American about our grocery industry. It is the envy of the world. As Americans, we absolutely take for granted our abundance and how it is on display in a grocery store. The freshness, quality, and an almost unimaginable variety of items are there to greet you. Our food supply is safe, convenient and cheap. Visiting Japanese are astounded by the low prices of our produce, meat and seafood. The Europeans think that the American focus on store cleanliness is bordering on obsession. To people living in third-world countries a trip to a modern Kroger store would be mind-boggling. It would leave them in awe of the American food distribution system and our abundance (both the good and the bad).

Now add to this mix, the element of added convenience to your everyday life. Reflect for a moment on how handy the in-store pharmacy, bank, and the bakery departments are to you. Yes, we have evolved <u>way beyond</u> grocery stores to supermarkets. We shop at these stores every week. They are an essential part of our lives and something we really don't think about in our busy world.

Grocery stores by many measures define excellence. The biggest grocers including Kroger, Albertson's, Safeway and the Ahold Group (Stop n Shop, Bi- Lo, Tops, Giant, Hannaford, etc) can astound us with their efficiency and 80,000 square foot shrines to food retailing. These are all huge corporations with annual sales in the many tens of billions of dollars. They are self-sufficient and vertically integrated. They own their own warehouses and distribution systems and in some cases even their own food manufacturing plants. They have also become much larger and even more efficient through industry consolidation. The big fish have gobbled up the little fish. The big national players have purchased many of the regional ones. In 2003, the 10 largest grocers represented about 60% of the business vs. just 37% in 1992[11].

On the other end of the spectrum are the small independent grocers. There are over 10,000 independent grocers in America today. Often their first or last name is the marquee on the store: Bob's Market. These local grocers represent a proud lot of independent businessmen who operate their own stores. They often align themselves in co-operative ventures (IGA being the largest) or with large food wholesaler distributors. The niche they fill is often defined in their ability to better serve their local customers, and communities than the big chains. The slogan of IGA is "Hometown Proud" and they do an admirable job in a tough environment. They often know their shoppers by name. In some cases families have shopped at "Bob's" IGA for multiple generations. Bob is part of the community; he coaches the soccer team, is on the board the local not-for-profit organization and is a member of your church congregation. Bob is not part of some "corporation".

In many ways the American grocery industry reflects what's best about American business. It is highly efficient and automated, with information systems and distribution systems that are state-of-the art. It can also be highly entrepreneurial as in the case of the independents and small chains. Even from a financial perspective the grocery industry has something that so many other industries are starved for – CASH. Perhaps the ultimate barometer of a company's health is its cash flow. While it is true that grocery profit margins are very thin, grocery stores generate a lot of cash.

The grocery industry also has a very proud heritage. As an industry, growth exploded in the generation following World War Two. In fact, from 1958-1967, supermarket sales increased 50%[12]. This was the golden age of the grocery store. It was the era where the rules were established and the "winning formulas" for success were set in stone.

In a nutshell here was the winning formula.

- Select prime store locations and know your shoppers
- Offer fresh produce and great variety
- Offer "hot deals" to draw in shoppers every week

This winning formula seemed to be invincible.

- The population was growing and as a result, there was an annual, built-in, growth factor.

- The business was thought to be inflation proof. When inflation increases, no problem, prices could be raised and passed on to the shopper.
- And above all else, there wasn't much competition for the food dollar?

The financial model associated with the winning formula seemed equally invincible. In general, here is a simple way to think about that model. There are three basic components.

- <u>Costs</u>: The primary costs in the grocery industry are warehousing (i.e. inventory), distribution, and operating the stores themselves (with labor being the single largest component).
- <u>Mark-up</u>: This is the difference between what products were purchased for – from food manufacturers and farmers - and sold for. Example: Kroger buys Kellogg's Corn Flakes from Kellogg's for $3 a box and sells them to their shoppers for $3.89 a box. The mark-up is 89 cents.
- <u>Profit</u>: This is the difference between mark-up and costs. Example: If it costs Kroger an average of 59 cents a box to warehouse, distribute and employ people to sell those Corn Flakes, their profit would be 89 cents less 59 cents = 30 cents profit.

In simplest of terms, grocery items are marked up about 26-28% on average. This covers the costs of doing business, which averages about 22-24%, and this leaves a 4% profit margin[13]. A 4% profit margin is "thin", but again, the cash flow associated with the operation is healthy.

The winning formula in review:

- Buy prime store locations – suburbia is ideal
- Offer tremendous variety and wholesome foods
- Advertise weekly hot deals to draw your shoppers in and communicate via newspapers
- Keep growing with the population
- Raise prices to stay ahead of inflation and pass the costs on to shoppers

- Mark merchandise up to cover costs and leave some for profit.
- Plow some of the profits into buying new stores, in prime suburban locations, and let the cycle repeat itself.
- Hire people to bag groceries, cut meat and check people out. Give them minimal annual increases.

Is this a self-perpetuating success engine or what? This is *THE* winning formula if there ever was one. This seemed invincible and set in stone.

Consider:

- The Heritage - 50% growth rates in one decade alone
- The cash flow - excellent
- The Logic (i.e. people *have to eat*).

What could possibly go wrong with this!?

The grocery industry became the classic "Frog in the pot". A very large, old, and comfortable frog.

Enter the old adage "Nothing fails like Success".

Enter Sam Walton and a new business model.

Enter the fact that shoppers like "everyday low prices"

Sam Walton changed the rules of the game and built a new winning formula.

Here are the facts:

- By 2002, Wal*Mart had become the largest grocer in the U.S. with sales of $58 Billion, surpassing Kroger ($48 billion), Albertson's ($36 billion) and Safeway ($32 billion).
- By the end of 2002 there were over 1,400 Wal*Mart Supercenters (i.e. Wal*Marts that also sell groceries).
- Not only have the big boys been passed, the smaller, independent grocers, have been particularly hard hit (e.g. 4th quarter 2001, 20% of Wal*Mart growth came at the expense of the top 10 chains and 80% came at the expense of the smaller retailers[14]).

Nobody in their wildest dreams would have imagined that this could have happened. But it did happen, and only in one decade, because Sam Walton built a better mousetrap.

To follow is the Grocery industry's winning formula and how Wal*Mart rewrote all the rules:

- Grocery - Buy prime store locations in suburbia because that's where the people are.
- W*M - Buy much less expensive real estate in rural/semi-rural areas and the people will drive to you.
- Grocery - Offer tremendous variety and wholesome foods. W*M - 1) Offer only the top selling food items as stocking "slow movers" causes enormous inefficiencies in the supply chain which drives operating costs up and, 2) redefine "tremendous variety" from just food to food AND General Merchandise (i.e. toothpaste, light bulbs, school supplies, etc – all the items that are in a typical Wal*Mart).
- Grocery - Advertise weekly hot deals to draw shoppers in and communicate via newspapers.
  W*M – offer the same low prices everyday to draw people in while 1) avoiding disruptions in the supply chain and 2) eliminating weekly advertising costs.
- Grocery - Keep growing with the population.
  W*M – Execute a business plan that results in market share gains regardless of population trends.
- Grocery – Assume this is an inflation-proof business and pass the increases on to the shoppers.
  W*M – Do not pass increases on to shoppers. Instead, become more cost-efficient internally and work with vendors to lower overall costs.
- Grocery - Mark merchandise up to cover costs.
  W*M – Continually lower prices and pass the efficiencies on through to the shoppers. Note: Typical grocery mark-up is 26-28%, typical W*M mark-up about 18% (with the food portion of the product mix being even lower).
- Grocery - Plow some of the profits into buying new stores.

W*M – Build new stores about as fast as is humanly possible, and not necessarily in suburbia. One new store opening <u>every 36 hours</u> for the past five years!).

- Grocery - Hire people to bag groceries, cut meat and check people out. Give them minimal annual increases.
  W*M – Hire people and instill a culture of enthusiasm. Financially reward employees through profit sharing programs.

What is the bottom line? It's simple, consumers like lower prices and Wal*Mart offers the lowest prices. Shoppers have been voting with their feet.

- At last count, Wal*Mart now owns $67 Billion in annual food sales. These are sales that would have been overwhelmingly sold through grocery stores.
- In 1980, virtually all weekly shopping trips for food were to the supermarket (94%). By 2000, only 68% of shopping trips for food are to the supermarket (vs. W*M Supercenters (22%) and Convenience stores (10%)[15].

W*M has a more effective business model than the grocers - one where low prices drive enormous volume. A fast-nickel is more profitable than a slow dime.

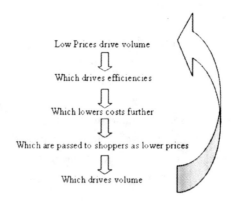

Low Prices drive volume
⇩
Which drives efficiencies
⇩
Which lowers costs further
⇩
Which are passed to shoppers as lower prices
⇩
Which drives volume

...........And so the productivity spiral continues.

So what has the grocery response been?

On the emotional front:

- Anger and frustration - Anger against Wal*Mart. In some cases, anger that a "birthright" has been taken from them and frustration that the winning formula no longer works.
- Denial - An unwillingness to admit that the temperature in the pot is getting as hot as it is.
- Rationalization – The thinking that things will eventually return to "normal".

On the business front:

Compared to the growth of Wal*Mart, the grocery response has been relatively weak and ineffective. Here are a few examples.

- Industry Consolidation – The large fish have swallowed the small fish in an effort to spread costs and be more efficient. Net result: they have not kept pace with Wal*Mart's growth and supply chain efficiencies, and in some cases, have lost touch with local market preferences in the process.
- Promotion Practices – The industry is still pushing weekly hot deals in an effort to drive store traffic. Net results – this practice continues to be 1) inefficient (as only a portion of the manufacturer's "deal money" actually gets passed to the consumer Vs. Wal*Mart passing all their money through), 2) disruptive to the supply chain and causing inefficiencies and 3) ineffective in increasing store shopper traffic which is either declining or not keeping pace with Wal*Mart[16].
- Buying Practices – The grocery industry, as a whole, has an antagonistic buying relationship with its vendors (e.g. the consumer packaged goods manufacturers). Net results: Communication and mutual problem solving are not at the same level with Wal*Mart.
- Employees – As an industry, Grocery employees continue to express high dissatisfaction with their jobs.
- Marketing – the large grocers have not formed a meaningful market niche, or brand, in the mind of the consumer. Not

only have they not created a unique position vs. Wal*Mart, they haven't established differentiation vs. each other. Net: Wal*Mart continues to establish its unique selling proposition in the mind of the consumer with" everyday low prices" while their competition becomes commodity-like.

As a quick mental check, consider this: pretend you have been blindfolded and led into a grocery store in another city. Now take the blindfold off and look around for a second. Do you know what grocery store you are in? I would suspect that in 95% of the cases you would not. Why? All grocery stores look alike because they basically *are* all alike. Now pretend the blindfold was removed and you were in a Wal*Mart. It would be suggested that you would know you were in a Wal*Mart within 1-5 seconds. You would have the same experience in a Target store, a Whole Foods Market or a Trader Joe's. They have all successfully differentiated themselves. The big grocers including Albertsons, Kroger and Safeway have not.

How boring have things become at the big grocers? Not only do they all look alike, they all stock the same items. Across eight core departments, Albertsons, Kroger and Safeway stock 28,584, 28,843 and 28,693 items respectively[17]. Amazing. They couldn't be more alike if they tried. All alike, and competing on price. That is the precise definition of a commodity.

As an aggregate, how far has the grocery industry fallen? In 2003, for the first time ever, shoppers made more visits to supermarkets for fill-in trips than stock-up trips[18].

For the grocery industry, this is a very dangerous position to be in. Here's why:

- It all comes down to branding. If there is no meaningful difference between your brand versus the competition in the mind of the shopper (the only place where a brand exists), they won't pay more for your products.
- By definition then the product is a commodity.
- If the product is a commodity then the only way to differentiate Vs the competition will be price.

- If the brand is competing on price, and Wal*Mart is the competition, then you lose - plain and simple.

Respected industry consultant, Art Turlock, articulates these circumstances as "the death spiral of the supermarket format". At a recent industry conference Turlock described the death spiral as follows:

Consolidation and leveraged buying have produced look-alike stores, while the marketplace is becoming more diverse. Supermarkets, occupying the undifferentiated middle ground, are losing relevance, and alternative formats are filling the gap. Manufacturers, meanwhile, are seeking more efficient channels for their trade dollars, so supermarkets will have to raise prices to make up for the lost trade money, and in the end, will run themselves out of business.

Fighting Back

So what should grocers do to thrive and survive under these circumstances?

The **FIRST** thing to do is to face reality. Face the reality that the heat has been turned up dramatically and that the "winning formulas" must be re-examined.

Albertsons CEO, Larry Johnston (formerly of General Electric), offers up a good example for other grocers to follow with this quote, "We blamed our fiscal shortfalls on new competitors, difficult economic conditions, high-energy prices, mergers and a number of other conditions for our problem. Clinically speaking, we were in a state of denial. We conned ourselves into believing that, as grocery experts, we had a track record of doing things right for generations and that we would bounce back once things returned to 'normal.' Well the fact is: Things aren't going to return to normal."

L. Johnston, GMA Forum 2002.

You will notice in this quote that Johnston touches on all of the four pillars as follows:

- Perseverance – It will take an enormous amount of perseverance to get the grocery industry out of the hole they are in.
- Knowledge – He will leverage his knowledge gained through other industries.
- Risk – It was an enormous risk to openly address that real problem.
- Passion – This is a passionate statement given by a passionate man – nothing watered down about these words. This is NOT typical grocery executive-speak.

Acknowledging reality like Larry Johnston did is the right place to start.

The **SECOND** thing to do is forget about beating Wal*Mart at their own game. Trying to compete on price vs. Wal*Mart is a sure fire way to decrease market share and erode profit. Grocers will never have a more efficient operation than Wal*Mart. Not only does Wal*Mart have the most efficient operation, they are getting better at a faster rate. I'm not advocating that traditional grocers stop trying to become more efficient – they should. Good operators are constantly looking at ways to improve. However, trying to convince shoppers that your prices are less than Wal*Mart's is a fool's game.

As Chris Hoyt, from Reveries Magazine, brilliantly points out, not only is it folly, it is mathematically impossible. Specifically, Chris points out two simple facts 1) expenses must be less than product mark-up if a profit is to occur and 2) Wal*Mart's mark-up (22%) is ALREADY less than the expenses of all Albertsons, Kroger and Safeway (September 2004). Therefore it is mathematically impossible for grocery stores to compete with Wal*Mart on price.

The **THIRD** step that must be taken is to establish meaningful brand differentiation in the marketplace Vs. Wal*Mart and other grocery competitors and jump out of the pot.

Is anyone applying these three principles and actually succeeding? The answer is yes. Several major food retailers have differentiated themselves and are doing well. The leaders include Whole Foods Market, Costco, HEB (San Antonio), Giant Eagle (Pittsburgh), Publix (Florida and Georgia) and Trader Joe's.

Trader Joe's will be examined in more detail.

TRADER JOE'S (205 stores)

It is hard to find shoppers more loyal to a grocer than Trader Joe's. Their strategy is brilliant. What they are all about is offering an upscale and fun food experience at a reasonable price. Their people are great as well. Who brings all this value to you? Why Trader Joe himself of course. Well, not literally, but that is exactly how it feels to Trader Joe's shoppers. They are loyal to "him" and appreciate the great food finds "he" brings to them (i.e. unique products from around the world).

Shopping at Trader Joe's is a fun, upbeat, and quirky experience. You never know what exactly what you will find but it will be something interesting. Trader Joe's most famous find was two-buck-chuck - a quality California wine (sourced during the 2003 grape-glut). Another recent special was frozen pizza from Italy - only $6 dollars. Get them while supplies last. The in-store sampling kitchen, one of the best in the industry, makes the opportunity to taste the latest offerings readily available.

I was talking to a friend of mine in Laguna Beach recently who is a typical Trader Joe's fan. Jack shared that, *"last night we served crab cakes and wine that we purchased at Trader Joe's. It couldn't have cost more than $10. It was delicious".*

No doubt about it, Trader Joe's makes their shoppers feel smart. Trader Joe looks out for them and brings them wonderful things.

It all begins with committed people and Trader Joe's has them. They are friendly, knowledgeable and helpful. They taste EVERY SINGLE product they sell and if they don't like it, they don't stock it. These people also have strong financial incentives based on how well the store they work at is doing. Like Wal*Mart, Trader Joe's shares the wealth. This breeds very loyal people who are committed.

A sign in Trader Joe's tells what they are all about, "Don't have the time to search the world for exciting foods, enticing flavors and compelling prices? Don't worry; we've already done it for you".

Trader Joe's also does something that the big guys have all but forgotten. They not only sell food, they *romance the food they sell.* Which advertisement, taken from the in-store flyers, does a better job of actually making you want to buy something?

Trader Joe's – Headline: Fully Cooked Marinated Chicken Breasts – How Easy!! *"We've developed Marinated Chicken Breasts that have been brushed with a sweet and tangy Asian-style glaze, then grilled to perfection and then individually quick-frozen. These chicken breasts are moist, tender and oh so convenient"*

Safeway - *Frozen chicken breasts @4.49 lb.*

A typical grocer will only talk about price – and competing primarily on price is sure-fire disaster if the competition includes Wal*Mart.

A Trader Joe's radio ad is not easily forgotten either. They romance their special food finds until your mouth begins to water. At the very end the tag line is added, "available at Trader Joe's while supplies last".

Trader Joe's also has arguably the best private label products of anyone - anywhere. These are always made by "a famous name that we can't reveal". Brilliant strategy. As a result the Trader Joe's brand seems like so much more than "just private label". The quality is excellent and you just know that Trader Joe is giving you great value because "he" is like that. There is trust. Trust breed's loyalty. Loyalty increases market share and profit.

Trader Joe's is also extremely efficient as follows:

- Stores are small and manageable, and with their limited assortment, it's easier to keep in stock
- Their labor costs are low (and they are not union).

- They do not engage in price discounting of existing products. They run an every day low price strategy like Wal*Mart, but with a unique set of items. As a result they cannot be compared directly with what Wal*Mart carries.
- Advertising costs are kept low because their word of mouth advertising is so strong.
- The Trader Joe's brand represents the majority of the products sold and generates high profits and loyalty.
- Their best kept secret is that they are owned by the ultra-efficient, and private, German company ALDI.

How are they doing financially? From 2001 through 2004, their compound annual growth rate was a whopping 15.1%[19].

How have they built such a successful business? Their secret is that they have **successfully differentiated themselves** in the market.

The bottom line is this, the grocers that don't change by effectively distinguishing themselves will continue to lose market share. Only the smartest grocers will be able to thrive. However, for those that take calculated risks, they will not only survive, but thrive.

Conversations with Dr. Fickeler

As usual, my conversations with Dr. Fickeler were quite revealing. It was fascinating to gain the insights of a professional who had both studied risk and who had practical industry experience as well.

Our conversations about risk could be categorized into three categories:

- The connection between risk and an individual's personality
- The personality of an organization
- The traditional association between risk and something negative.

Risk and Personality

When it comes to risk-taking, it's highly personal. It depends on the individual. Risk-taking is as unique as individuals and everyone has a unique propensity to define and accept risks. What is within one person's comfort zone may be too risky for somebody else.

Some researchers in the field of psychology have actually assigned five factors to personality. If you have studied psychology you may recognize this as the Big Five Theory of personality. The five factors are:

- Extroversion
- Agreeableness
- Conscientiousness
- Neuroticism
- Openness to Experience

Other researchers will argue that there is actually a "6th" factor: <u>risk-taking</u>. Risk-taking is that important to an individual's personality.

The more you learn about the connection between risk-taking and personality the more interesting it becomes. For some people risk-taking is a necessity. They actually *need* to take risks. For these people, risk taking is like a high, which they seek. Risk taking can cause a physiological reaction, which causes the nervous system to become stimulated. Their heart rate may increase. Some people may literally have "the need for speed". Others may have a need to seek adventure or even the sick need to excessively gamble. These people feel they have to take risks just to feel comfortable.

Other people have a very different comfort zone and will have very different reactions to the same stimuli. With these people, the same events can trigger the opposite of a high – they will feel fear or apprehension. These people are literally afraid to take risks.

The bottom line is that different personality types can have dramatically different reactions to the same set of stimuli.

To better understand how people <u>view</u> risks differently, consider the following group exercise.

<u>First</u>: Have people write down the biggest risks they have taken in the last 3 years and how they would rate that degree of risk on a 10-point scale.

<u>Second</u>: Ask the participants to describe their risks (but without divulging their rating)

<u>Third</u>: Get feedback from the group as to how they would rate those same risks.

What you will consistently find is that the people who took the largest risks (according to the balance of the group) did not rate the risk nearly as high on their own scale. To them, it wasn't a risk as much as it was an extension of a passion or a talent or a skill. Sometimes, activities like skydiving, singing the National Anthem at the ballpark, or mountain climbing – things that most people would describe as risky - are described in casual terms by the people who have actually done them.

Ultimately, what makes some people risk takers and some not, is based on 1) how they are hard-wired (i.e. their genetic makeup), 2) the experiences they have had in their lives, and 3) the circumstances in which they find themselves.

Circumstances have a very direct, and obvious, bearing on risk-taking. People will take more risks as their circumstances change. Consider this situation and answer this question: would any "normal" person walk over a tightrope strung between two buildings 200 feet above the ground? Absolutely not! Now let's throw in a little wind, some rain and a bunch of screaming people. The answer would still be definitely no. Now let's change the circumstances. Now consider that the tightrope is the ONLY route to rescue between you and your child. In other words, if you can't reach your child via the tightrope, the child will die. Now what do you do? If you are a parent, there is nothing to decide – you go.

Now let's consider a circumstance that is a little more realistic. What if your company decided to eliminate half of its workforce and the employees were told they would have to "interview" for the remaining jobs to have a chance of being retained? How would these circumstances impact the individual employees to take risks? Each employee would strongly desire one of the remaining positions. Resources would be scarce and people would be scared of losing their jobs. This type of circumstance would drive people to extreme risk-taking to save their job. In evolutionary terms, when resources are scarce, competition for those resources increases.

Risk and Its Relevance to Organizations

Just as individuals have differing views on what a risk really is, so do organizations. Organizations can influence a person's behavior based on the organization's level of comfort with risk, their risk propensity, the level at which they assess risks, and if they view risks as positive or negative. A great risk-taker in an organization will have their ideas squelched simply if the organization doesn't condone or promote risk taking. Just as researchers in this area see risk-taking as a negative quality, most organizations still tend to see risk-taking behavior as a negative, and not a positive, quality. If you reward people based on outcomes rather than a process, they will engage in greater risk-taking behavior. Until organizations see risk-taking as a positive quality, creativity and innovation will suffer, because it is the risk-takers of today that are already planning for tomorrow.

Why so Negative?

The word "risk" has different meanings to different people. For some, risk is associated with fear, a gamble, or the possibility of getting hurt. With others, risk equals the opportunity to be first and to succeed. In short, the definition of risk is as unique as people are. When risk is researched within the context of "the scientific literature", the majority of articles have a negative connotation. Volumes have been written about risk within the context of drug and alcohol use, sexual health issues and gambling. It would therefore be logical to assume that the majority of researchers studying risk-taking see it as a negative quality as well.

It's time for a paradigm shift in this thinking. It is time that organizations turn that negative connotation generally associated with risk taking into a positive.

For organizations and businesses to be successful in the future, they will have to reposition the meaning of risk. Within the context of delivering innovation, risk-taking must be seen as a skill. Skills of course are associated with something that is positive. Risk-taking is a skill to be honed not a negative to be avoided. Skill is associated with talent and talent is what all companies need to drive innovation. Appropriate risk-taking is what companies must now recruit for, condone, and reward.

Companies need to develop new attitudes as it relates to risk. In short, they need to develop a <u>culture of courage</u> when it relates to how they view risk. This is good news. Like all skills, risk-taking can be honed (in individuals and in organizations). This is good news. Yes, some people are born with more skill than others, but everyone can increase their skills through diligence. It is a choice.

Chapter 6 Key Learning

- The connotations associated with risk are slowly changing from being exclusively negative.
- There is great danger in not changing and adjusting to the new realities in the environment.
- Risk is an essential ingredient in the innovation process.
- A "Culture of Courage" must be adapted.
- Business, like nature, abhors a vacuum. If there is a new and better mousetrap to be made, somebody will do it. The question is, will it be your organization or your competitor who does the innovating?

Something to Think About…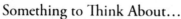

- Has an organization you have worked for, or an industry you have worked in, behaved like the frog in the pot?
- Are you aware of others who have "managed" their careers, marriage, or life like the frog in the pot?
- Have you ever been the frog in the pot, and if so, why did you stay?
- What are some of the consequences of "staying in the pot"?

Self-help for Risk Taking:
Your 90-Day Prescription

1. Consider this quote, "*Security is mostly a superstition. It does not exist in nature. Avoiding danger is no safer in the long run than outright exposure. Life is either a daring adventure or nothing at all*"
Helen Keller

Wow. What a powerful quote. Helen Keller was right. Pursuing security will only prove futile and unfulfilling. The frog in the pot had deluded itself.

<u>**Perspective to be gained**</u>: Security <u>doesn't truly exist;</u> it's an illusion. Instead pursue a full life that entails a certain degree of natural risk. You may not want to put yourself in a position where you are old and gray and say, "I wish I would have…….." This is a common tragedy and almost always manifests itself in insufficient risk-taking.

2. Ask yourself, "What am I really afraid of?" and then make a list. In many cases it's not snakes, terrorists or even death that we are afraid of. I am convinced that 99% of our fears will never, EVER, be realized. Winston Churchill may have said it best, "we have nothing to fear but fear itself". So what are we most typically afraid of day-in and day-out? It's usually some form of social rejection. Here are some thoughts to consider on this subject. Consider that 99% of the time people are not thinking about you, your career, your life or the meaning of your words. The sad truth is most of the time people aren't even listening to what you are saying. What are they thinking about? - Their life, their problems, their careers, etc. Don't worry about being judged by others, in today's society nobody cares or has the time. Shakespeare said it best, "*To thine own self be true*".

<u>**Exercise to perform:**</u> Summon the courage and develop the habit to "ask forgiveness and not permission". Do this at least once a week and <u>see what happens</u>. You will find that *nothing happens*. You will not be judged or criticized. You will find that people will either respect you for being proactive and being yourself or they will be ambivalent.

3. **Lifestyle change to make - Cultivate new friendships**. Get out and make some new acquaintances. Sometimes to gain new perspectives and expand your thinking you need to make some new friends. Spend more time with new and different people. Ask any tennis player what they need to do to get better and they will say, "play with someone who is better than I am". The same thing is true when it comes to developing risk taking skills. To get better, it helps to associate with some different people. Stand back from your "comfortable friends" for a minute and look around. Ask yourself who are those people who just exude self-confidence and seem to look at risk-taking differently than I do? You will find in many cases that these people have been freed from their own fears somewhere along the way and that their presence will in turn liberate you. Seek their presence.

Consider these words: *"I've been doing all my life after people who interest me, because the only people for me are the mad ones, the ones who are mad to live, mad to talk, mad to be saved, desirous of everything at the same time, the ones who never yawn or a say a commonplace thing, but burn, burn, burn, like fabulous yellow roman candles"*

Jack Kerouac <u>On The Road</u>

The types of people Kerouac describes are not those who seek to avoid risks, but rather those who embrace life. After you get to know some perceived risk-takers you will discover an amazing thing about them. You will come to realize that risk-taking is entirely relative. In other words what *most people* perceive as a risk they do not. This is because they have developed their risk-taking muscles to the point to where the job is not perceived as risky to them. You can do the same.

4. **Book to Read:** *<u>The Last Word on Power</u>* by Traci Goss. This book was marketed as a business book "for leaders who must make the impossible happen". The themes in the book however are far more universal than business. The central themes are 1) dying to self (and our fears) in the same way that the ancient samurai warriors would prior to going into battle and 2) making "bold promises" about a future that is our responsibility to create.

5. **<u>Movie to watch</u>**: *Erin Brockovich*

Chapter Seven – Passion

"We may affirm that absolutely nothing great in the world has been accomplished without passion"

George Hegel

"There is real magic in enthusiasm. It spells the difference between mediocrity and accomplishment."

Norman Vincent Peale

"No great thing was ever achieved without enthusiasm"
                                                    Emerson

*"It is not the critic who counts: The credit belongs to the man who
is actually in the arena, whose face is marred by dust and sweat
and blood, who strives valiantly, who errs and comes up short
again and again, who spends himself for a worthy cause; who,
at the best, knows, in the end, the triumph of high achievement,
and who, at the worst, if he fails, at least he fails while daring
greatly, so that his place shall never be with those cold and timid
souls who knew neither victory nor defeat."*
                                            Theodore Roosevelt 1910

*"You are either an energy-giver or an energy-taker. Surround
yourself with energy-givers."*
                                                    Randy Rose

"You can't start a fire without a spark"
                                            Bruce Springsteen

Webster's definition:

Pas-sion (n): 1) emotions as distinguished from reason and 2) an
    intense, driving or overmastering feeling or conviction and 3)
    a strong liking or desire for or devotion to some activity, object
    or concept.

There are some common themes running through these quotes and
the official Webster definition.

- Passion is separate from reason.
- Passion is inseparable from extraordinary achievement
- Passion is more than a spark; it's a fire!

Passion is also the foundation on which all the other pillars are
built. Passion is the indispensable ingredient that allows everything
else to happen. It is a deep rooted, and strong, desire to achieve or to

make something happen. Dreams do not come true without passion. Passion can be overpowering in good ways or bad. It can be maniacal, obsessive, and irrational – but above all it is undeniable. It is present in all people who have built something of significance. Passion is a burning, unquenchable *drive*.

The greatest of all time exuded passion:

- Van Gogh
- Elvis Presley
- Dr. Martin Luther King, Jr.
- Babe Ruth
- Mother Theresa
- John F Kennedy
- Tiger Woods
- Mick Jagger
- Vince Lombardi
- Jesus
- FDR
- Joan of Arc
- Gandhi
- Ernest Hemmingway
- Eleanor Roosevelt
- Louie Armstrong
- Abraham
- Michael Jordan
- Secretariat
- Muhammed Ali
- Henri the 8th

Now think for a moment about the individuals we have reviewed in this book. People like Swede Momsen, Thomas Edison and Sam Walton. Steven Jobs and Burt Rutan (winner of the space travel X Prize) have passion. The great ones, the ones who made a difference, all had enormous passion.

The good news is that most everyone is passionate about something. My 7-year-old son, Robbie, is passionate about basketball. He has red hair and freckles and he is an explosion of energy. Robbie is a blur.

Robbie has already informed the family that he is going to North Carolina where he will play college basketball. He has also shared with us that, "I will not be doing any homework in college because college is for basketball". It began with the movie <u>Space Jam.</u> In this movie, Michael Jordan leads a cast of misfit cartoon characters to an upset victory over space alien ball players (of course!). We bought the videotape. We wore that tape out – literally. He practiced his Michael Jordan slam dunk on his Little Tykes basketball hoop obsessively. He has watched countless NBA highlight films, including the individual highlight films of Pete Marovich, Larry Bird and Wilt Chamberlain. He wore those out. Robbie has basketball posters and pennants in his room and a full-size cut out of a 7' tall NBA payer. He plays basketball video games. He has a Michael Jordan jersey among many. He plays on multiple teams including the YMCA Hoopsters. He has developed a decent crossover dribble and no-look pass. Last year during one of his games (in which I was refereeing and coaching) I had to stop the game to chastise my own son for trash talking!!

We go to high school, college and pro games together. He begs me, or his mother, to apply those kids "tattoos" to his arms, "So I can be like the NBA players". He cries when it's time to stop playing. He cries if he loses a game of "h-o-r-s-e". He has a passion for the game. Robbie is 3' 11" tall and weighs 49 pounds. God bless him.

Passion is different from all the other Pillars

Passion is also different because it is the hardest to learn. The word passion is a noun. It is a thing. In general it is a thing that people either have or do not have.

The following can be learned or can be conjured up through force of will:

- Knowledge – the combination of formal education and informal experience.
- Perseverance – if you want to badly enough, you can persevere.
- Risk – a conscious choice

- Leadership – it's not a birthright – it can be taught, learned and honed.

But passion is different – you can't fake passion!

This is why it's so important that we follow our passions and that we encourage our children to do the same. Truly succeeding in life and career without following our true passion is akin to finding true love in an arranged marriage. It might happen but it's not likely. The rooster crows because he is passionate about the sun coming up. You can't sneak the sun past him, nor can you expect the "cows to crow" because they just aren't too passionate about it.

In some cases passion is the result of something that has happened in the past. It might be something deeply profound that has touched you. A psychologist might refer to this as a "significant emotional event". In the case of Swede Momsen, it was very likely a significant emotional event that triggered his passion. Was it that horrible feeling of helplessness in seeing "the bubbles come up" from the sunken sub, but knowing there was nothing he could do? Was that the spark that caused him to pursue his life-saving contraptions for several decades?

In the movie, The Silence of the Lambs, was Dr. Hannibal Lechter right? Was it the murder of Clarice Starling's policeman father, combined with her inability to stop the slaughter of the lambs on a farm as a child that led to her choice of a career in law enforcement? I surely haven't a clue, and I'm not a psychologist, but it sure seems to fit.

In other cases, it appears that passion is something that you are just born with. In some people, passion surfaces as a musical talent. Their passion is expressed through their music. We could all cite numerous examples of passionate musical prodigies.

From Justin Timberlake to Cardboard Boxes

One of the more interesting examples is Justin Timberlake. You may recognize him as, ex-pop idol, the lead singer in the boy's band N*SYNC and perpetrator of the infamous "wardrobe malfunction" during the 2004 Super Bowl halftime show. Of course there was a time when all 11 year-old girls recognized Justin Timberlake. Or as my daughter Madeline once said, "If they don't Dad, then there must be something wrong in their minds".

Whether you love this guy or hate him, there is no denying his talent. As a two year-old, his mother and siblings were amazed by his ability to seemingly sing along with the radio and move to the beat. As a third-grader young Justin organized a boys singing troupe for a talent night at school. To say he stole the show would be a gross understatement. Not only did he gyrate and primp on stage, with microphone in hand, but he also had all the eight year old girls shrieking and squealing. You would have thought it was the second coming of the Beetles or maybe Elvis himself. If you ever get a chance to see that home video you will be amazed. Justin Timberlake later went on to become a Disney Mouseketeer. His audition song? Some schmaltzy kid's tune? No. Justin Timberlake belted out a passionate version of the Percy Sledge classic When a Man Loves a Woman. The talent scouts and judges were stunned. They were universally amazed at the boy's immense charisma and talent. Whether you love or hate him, it must be agreed that Justin Timberlake was born with a passion, recognized it early and followed that passion to great success.

Remember, passion cannot be faked. In the case of musical performers, the audience can always tell the difference. Audiences will be attracted too and pay more for performances that reflect passion. They instinctively can sense it. The same is true in your life. Tap into your passion!

A key to driving innovation in the business world is aligning the passion of your people with the work to be done. Don't hire people who aren't passionate about what they are doing. More about this is chapter 8.

The Flame Burning Within

The mental model for Passion is a flame burning from within.

A flame is an excellent metaphor for passion. True passion is something that burns from within. It is the source of internal drive. It is like the fuel for your own internal combustion engine.

- Passion does not sit on the fence. Passion jumps over the fence, crawls under it or runs through it.
- Passion is contagious.
- Passion is the key ingredient that allows everything else to happen. A chemist would refer to passion as the catalyst.

A chef might say that it's the flame – or heat - that is the key to cooking. You can have the best food ingredients, the best pots, pans, knives and ovens, and even your grandmother's favorite recipe – but with no flame – with no heat – you have nothing. You will only have half-baked ideas and cold soup. And in my opinion, soup was NEVER meant to be served cold.

Passion is often described in terms of being hot. Certainly this is the case when Hollywood gets involved, but it is also true for innovation purposes. Passion is that inner source of heat that keeps you alive in a cold, indifferent, and unbelieving world. It keeps your dreams alive when others throw cold water on them. Passion is what allows others to catch fire and see your vision.

Our story of passion in the business world involves a company called Wilton Connor Packaging. Like the last chapter, it would have been easy to use a famous business example like Wal*Mart and Sam Walton, or Microsoft and Bill Gates. But that would too redundant. You are already familiar with what they built and how they did it. In The Power to Innovate we wanted to offer up fresh examples that would not only stimulate the intellect but touch your heart. With Wilton Connor Packaging we will go straight to the heart. Wilton Connor Packaging (WCP), founded by Wilton Connor of course, is one of the most successful companies that you have never heard of. Wilton Connor himself is a Horatio Alger American success story if there ever was one. Like Sam Walton, Wilton Connor didn't make his fortune in microchips, telecommunications, or oil. Wilton made his fortune, and left his mark on thousands of lives, by selling cardboard. He also did it with a passion and unrivaled flair.

Located in Charlotte, N.C., WCP is arguably the most successful corrugate display building company in the world. In simplest terms, WCP produces cardboard displays for retail stores as well as packaging for the products that are sold in them. In a nutshell, they add value to cardboard. Some examples include.

- Product packaging
- Back-to-school displays
- Christmas Displays
- Valentines Displays
- Special/Customized Events

WCP takes corrugated cardboard and print it, cut it, fold it and glue it into thousands of innovative display concoctions or product packages. Their innovative and customized display pieces for example – from Back-to-school School Buses full of batteries to a Pet Snack "choo-choo train" (complete with engine and caboose of course) reflects their passion, innovation and creativity.

Their clients include Procter and Gamble, Black & Decker, Nestle Purina Pet Care, Sunoco, Eveready Battery, Wal*Mart, Target, etc. In 2002, WCP generated over $60 million in sales and employed over

500. They boast a modern 25- acre campus that includes over two million square feet of manufacturing and warehouse space.

How did this company start? It all started with one man with a vision, and a dollar in his pocket in 1988.

Wilton Connor: Courtesy of Wilton Connor

To follow is Wilton Connor's story. Wilton Connor had been working in the industry for 18 years before he started his own company. He had multiple experiences, including working for several different companies and moving several times. The first five years of his career were spent in customer service, at the lowest level at the factory. It was in this environment that he learned the basics of the business including the product knowledge details. After his stint at the factory he went on the road as a salesman and developed a successful track record. His success was noticed and he was promoted to District Sales manager and transferred to an aging plant in Philadelphia. Wilton was not exactly met with open arms. The day he arrived, three salesmen quit because they thought that they should have had his job. It was at this old plant that Wilton learned what not to do. As Wilton said, "it was a learning experience". This was not a good plant. They did not have good quality, good ethics or a good spirit. In addition, the plant scheduler drank his lunch. He was usually fine in the morning, but pretty well sauced by noon. Wilton learned to work around the man and actually began doing his scheduling for him. Things began to change. Morale improved, delivery improved and the plant stopped losing accounts.

Wilton's work was recognized and he was promoted and moved again, this time as the Sales Manager of the Baltimore plant. It was in Baltimore that Wilton's product, operations and sales knowledge deepened. One of his more memorable experiences came from working with Procter and Gamble. P&G wanted fully-formed boxes shipped to their blow-molded bottle suppliers. The suppliers would then insert the empty bottles and ship them back to P&G for filling and distribution to retail. Since P&G had multiple suppliers of bottles (who were hostile to each other) it made sense to ask the box company to erect the boxes and ship them to the various bottle manufacturers empty. This practice was highly unusual at the time as box manufacturers only shipped "flat boxes". They never shipped ones that were already constructed. What Wilton learned from this experience though was invaluable. Wilton learned that an outstanding company like P&G was <u>willing to pay for</u> one-source solutions.

Wilton Connor then left that company after 13 years and went to work for a competitor in his hometown of Charlotte. The man who originally hired Wilton had hired him away. He asked Wilton, "how would you like to move back home, become a sales manager and within two years become General Manager?" It sounded great but it turned out to be nightmare. It was hell. To quote Wilton, "the man I worked for hated me and I hated him". He blocked Wilton's efforts at every turn. Wilton came to hate his job so intensely that he would get sick every morning before going to work. He had three small children a house payment and a car payment. He wanted out.

One morning Wilton approached the man and said, "This isn't working out, just put me on the road and let me sell". The man gave Wilton the worst territory imaginable, one with few cities or customers! He then said to him, "I hope you fail". But Wilton Connor did not fail. In fact, within 18 months he was selling over half of the plant's production. But he still wanted out.

It was at this time that he got his big chance. Wilton had begun to cultivate a relationship with Eveready Battery. What Eveready wanted was for someone to produce erected boxes that could be filled with batteries and then sent on to their retailers. Of course this all sounded familiar to Wilton and he knew it could be done. The problem though was that his existing company didn't want anything to do with the project. The demand was there though and Wilton knew what the customer needed. Eveready didn't want to run the equipment in plant but they were willing to purchase the equipment and lease it to someone who would do it for them. The lease price was one dollar. Wilton Connor thought to himself, – "I have a dollar". He quit his job and started his own company. That was in 1988.

The early years were extraordinarily difficult. Even though Wilton did "have a dollar", what was really at stake financially was <u>cash flow</u> (i.e. the ability to pay his suppliers and employees while waiting to be paid). To keep his new company afloat, Wilton took all of his family savings, sold his IRA's, and double mortgaged his house. It still wasn't enough. He didn't qualify for a line of credit at the bank. What he and his wife ended up doing was using 36 Visa and Master Cards. It was the only money they could get! They almost went bankrupt three times.

If cash flow wasn't the only thing to worry about, there was also an acute labor shortage in Charlotte in 1988. Charlotte was booming and everyone was employed. The only labor Wilton could find was Vietnamese. The only reason that the Vietnamese weren't employed was because they often didn't speak *any* English. At first, Wilton and his employees shared only one common word, "O.K." Through a combination of hand signals and "O.K.'s", Wilton Connor and his employees were able to look at the diagrams and pictures together and agree on the work to be done.

During these first two years, Wilton used his sales skills like never before. He would have to constantly convince his suppliers, his employees and his customers to hang in there. And hang in there they did. Wilton knew through experience that successful selling was directly related to:

1. People liking you
2. Having outstanding product knowledge
3. Filling their needs by being a great listener

The first part came naturally to him. Wilton Connor is simply one of the most caring, enthusiastic and likable people you would ever want to meet. His friends and peers describe him as a "sales evangelist". Watching Wilton in front of a customer is truly watching a master craftsman at his trade.

Wilton's caring for other human beings is also legend. So much so that he was featured on the ABC's Nightline Magazine. One of the themes of the feature was how WCP treated his employees differently. For example, in addition to their wages, Wilton's employees are also provided with some rather unusual benefits including:

- A free home-cooked meal everyday. I have eaten these on several occasions and they are excellent.
- Free shuttle service to and from work.
- A free-handy man to work on their homes when they are away working (WCP supplies the handyman and the employee supplies the materials).
- Laundry service was available at $1 a load. Yes, they do ironing too!

To say that Wilton Connor's employees are loyal would be a gross understatement. They love this guy and would do anything for him. The old saying, "I don't care how much you know until I know how much you care" describes Wilton. His employees know that they are valued.

Quite frankly, Wilton is very humble and trying to get some of these stories out of him is like pulling teeth. He keeps deflecting all the glory and credit to others. Here is the story though that I like the most. One day, Wilton and I were walking through his facilities when a young Hispanic worker looks up from his work and shouts out, "Mr. Wilton!" All the other workers look up at Wilton with the same broad smile and look of gratitude. I had to ask, "Wilton, what was that all about?" "Oh, that's Jose" said Wilton. "Well what about Jose?" I said, prying a bit more. "Well Jose had been deaf since birth and had never heard his own name. His Doctor in Mexico told his parents that he would always be deaf. Long story short, we took him to the leading specialist in Charlotte who performed a new procedure and now Jose can hear". You don't have to convince the employees at WCP that Mr. Wilton has passion - and compassion.

Wilton also has extraordinary product knowledge that reflects a lifetime of doing. This knowledge allows him to lead and innovate with confidence. He knows the details. There may be no one on earth who knows more about how to add value to corrugated paper products. One of the best examples of this comes from one of Wilton's own customers, a Mr. Scott Scardino, Sr. Sales Manager, from one of WCP's customers. When Scott was a rookie box salesman he asked Wilton to accompany him on a call to a manufacturer of electric blankets. This manufacturer was considering upgrading their packaging. Scott vividly recalled how the buyer was tremendously impressed with Wilton "With one quick look at the package they were currently using, Wilton was able to tell him precisely how the package was constructed and handled in their plant". Wilton then went on to spell out all the details. He then told the manufacturer, "we want to design a package for you that's 1) more attractive (and we'll come back with a mock-ups), and 2) that's easier to assemble. I'm assuming you have stations set up in-line where people are paid on a per production unit basis and then the blankets are manually folded, placed into bags the bags are l-bar sealed of course - then packed into the carton, which looks to be set up by hand." The manufacturer said, "You've been here five minutes and you knew all this just by looking at the box?"Scott recalls; "I was floored and the buyer was floored. The buyer's perspective was, this guy really knows his stuff and I'd be well advised to make him a part of what we do".

Of course much of what transpired in the example above was the result of Wilton being a passionate *listener*. As one of his own employees shared with me, "a big part of coming up with innovative solutions pertains to answering the need. This is far more than answering the question. Listening first is a key. I think some of WCP's best creative cooking has come about via heavy measures of the 'listening' ingredient".

The service of WCP is legendary. This testimonial from one of their very smallest customers will illustrate. "Dear Wilton, once again the response from your folks was outstanding! This small project to help our local retail specialists was handled with as much concern, spirit and professionalism as a multi-million dollar order. Alan also called me this morning with additional questions to make sure everything would be made perfect for the application. I'm not telling you anything you don't already know about your folks, but believe me the EXCELLENCE is recognized and very much appreciated".

We asked Wilton Connor a lot of questions in preparation of this book. In turn, he passed some of our questions on to his suppliers, customers and employees. What came through loud and clear was the conscientious nature of those responses. Most of them were several pages in length and the language was very thoughtful in its nature. You could tell that their relationship with WCP was deep, meaningful and based on respect. Their responses also clearly reflected WCP's passion. One of the responders shared that Wilton's passion was the key and that "passion is the mother of all invention". As was discussed earlier, passion is contagious and is never lukewarm!

So what is Wilton Connor doing right now? He just sold the other half of his company to a Fortune 100 company (the first half was sold in 1999). Wilton is now retired and doing important work in the community. He has amassed a large personal fortune but more importantly has hundreds of friends, fans and supporters around the globe. Not bad for someone in their mid-50's.

To summarize, Wilton Connor:

- Followed his passion
- Persevered through the early years
- Took enormous risks, and
- Had unsurpassed knowledge in his field.

Wilton Connor lived, and exuded, the four pillars of innovation.

Conversations with Dr. Fickeler

Jennifer performed perhaps her most exhaustive research literature review on the role that passion plays in innovation. Interestingly, few studies were found on what explicitly makes people passionate about something. What became evident was that each person is unique in what makes them passionate. It is part of a person's personality that makes them different. Where one person is passionate about art and therefore frequents art galleries and literature, another person is passionate about foreign languages and is bilingual. Our passions are what make us unique.

From an organizational standpoint, individual passions should be developed and used to help us utilize our skills and talents to the fullest. Think about any one of your passions for a moment. Reflect on how you feel when you are engaged in your passion interest. Imagine that you are passionate about golf. Perhaps you dream about the next time you play and are constantly trying to improve your game. You read books about the latest golf equipment and follow all the PGA tour events. When you are playing golf, you lose yourself in the time and nothing else seems to matters. This is passion!

In relation to organizations, if you are working on a project that you are excited about, you will constantly strive to do your best and you enjoy your work. Sometimes this is tough within a work setting because you might be involved in a project that is not exciting. However, an organization that tries to find ways to utilize those areas in which you are passionate will allow the worker to be more productive.

In addition to exploring individual passions, an organization can foster an environment where passion is connected directly to the work and the company. Jennifer recently attended a conference of industrial/organizational psychologists where a spokesperson discussed the corporate culture of JetBlue Airlines. The speaker discussed how the company was *founded* on the principle of passion. Passion is one of the top corporate values of JetBlue Airlines. These values are publicized in every office, on every plane ticket, and it is what their employees live and breathe. Airline employees, as a group, tend to be enthusiastic about flying and travel, and tend to spend their whole career in the industry. JetBlue seeks the most enthusiastic of an already passionate group. The speaker also mentioned how people were hired based on their acceptance of values. They hire and fire according to these values regardless of rank in the company. Consequently, JetBlue Airlines had the largest startup of any airline and turned a profit in the very first month of their existence. This is unheard of in the airline industry. JetBlue has only been in existence for two years. Their future will be most interesting to follow.

In reflecting on the JetBlue example, there are multiple opportunities for an organization to promote passion. For one, an organization's top executives must convey passion to the rest of the company. They must walk the walk and talk the talk. Most employees look to top management as an example to follow. Supervisors must provide an example of what the company should be. Management must lead through the way they conduct themselves. If an organization's President takes pride in his work, makes appearances at functions and gives encouragement, then the employees will feel the passion and follow suit. To demonstrate that passion is important, you need to make it a part of what employees live and breathe. It has to be represented in the values they espouse. It must become part of the organization's culture. The employees also need to know that there are consequences associated with not living up to these values. If they don't subscribe to the values or subscribe to the vision, the company must be willing to let them go or suffer the consequences.

In connecting all of these pillars, it is contended that passion is the piece de resistance of innovation. Passion allows an individual to persevere no matter what happens. Specialized knowledge is the result of what people enjoy reading about and exploring. People are also more likely to take a risk in an area that holds passion for them. Therefore, it is essential that organizations explore ways to allow individuals to exploit their passions.

How can organizations foster passion at work?

- Company leaders must exhibit passionate behavior
- Passionate behavior that leads to business success must be openly recognized and rewarded
- Make passion part of on the mission statement
- Recruit employees who demonstrate passion for the industry and for getting things done
- Make passion a priority through training

- Supervisors should seek to find the passions of their employees and then apply that passion towards the work that needs to be done. It is said that "Every employee comes with a set of operating instructions. It is the job of the supervisor to find them and take action".
- Develop a measurement for passion of the employees

Chapter 7 Key Learning

- Passion is an indispensable ingredient in the innovation process.
- Passion is the foundation on which the other pillars are built.
- Look for passion in those you hire and align that passion with the work to be done.
- Great things can be accomplished if you are passionate enough.

Something to Think About...

- What are you passionate about?
- What fires are burning within you?
- How do you best align your passion with your career and projects?

Self-help for Developing Passion:
Your 90-Day Prescription

• **Perspective to be gained:** Consider these great words and then ask yourself, "Who am I to *not* become much more passionate about what I believe in?"

Our worst fears are not that we are inadequate. Our worst fears are that we are powerful beyond measure. It is our light, not our darkness, that most frightens us. We ask ourselves, "Who am I to be brilliant, gorgeous, talented, and fabulous?" Actually, who are you not to be? You are a child of God; your playing small doesn't serve the world. There is nothing enlightened about shrinking so that other people won't feel insecure around you. We were born to make manifest the glory of God within us. It is not just in some of us, it is in everyone and as we let our light shine, we occasionally give other people permission to do the same. As we are liberated from our own fear, our presence automatically liberates others.

Nelson Mandela, Inaugural Speech 1995

• **Exercise to Perform:** Remember the U.S. Armed Services recruiting campaign that featured this as their tagline, "If a book were written about your life would anyone want to read it?" Of course, this question is the voiceover for dramatic scenes of young man and women jumping out of airplanes, repelling off cliffs and driving tanks. Pretty intense stuff. How about you? What in your life are you most passionate about? Write no more than one page on this subject with particular emphasis on how you feel about it (so much so that others would be able to feel the excitement and passion in your words). This doesn't have to be fancy, your one-pager could be about the passion you have for fly fishing. Now think about what you wrote and ask, "How could this apply to other areas of my life?"

The second exercise would be to make special weekly walks part of your health regimen. During these walks consciously use all of your senses in a new and powerful way to experience nature. Use your skill of imagination and pretend that you were just given a new lease on life.

Pretend that a doctor who had told you the day before that you had an inoperable disease, just called back and admitted to a terrible mistake! It wasn't you it was someone else. <u>Now</u> experience your nature walk like you never have before. Breathe in and savor the smells, the sounds of the birds, the wind and your own footsteps, and literally feel your walk as your feet touch the ground.

3. **<u>Lifestyle change to make</u>:** Make more acquaintances with people who are passionate. Their passion will rub off on you and will liberate you from your fears in the same way that risk-takers will.

4. **<u>Book to Read</u>:** *The Agony and the Ecstasy* by Irving Stone. This portrays the life and passion of Michelangelo.

5. **<u>Movie to watch</u>:** – <u>A Lust for Life</u> This is Kirk Douglas' Portrayal of Vincent van Gogh – his best movie ever? Play to Watch – Les Miserables.

Chapter Eight –
Nurturing Innovation in Your Organization

"Don't throw the baby out with the bathwater"
Common Wisdom

"You can't pull up the plant to see how the roots are growing"
Stephen Covey

"Thinking is the hardest work that man will ever do; and that is why so little of it is ever done"
Mark Twain

So how do you <u>not</u> throw out the baby, be patient with the progress of the crops and *really* think hard about nurturing innovation? It's not easy. In this chapter, and the two that follow, the focus will be on nurturing, separating the facts from the myths, and breaking down the barriers.

Structure for Innovation

The notion of structuring for innovation in organizations might seem counterintuitive. Innovation and organizational structure don't necessarily seem to go together, but they do. It's easy to think of innovation in terms of that which is free flowing, esoteric, or even evasive. Structure, on the other hand, implies rigidity. However, experience has consistently shown that all companies, organizations (and even individuals) are perfectly structured to get the results that they do. Not only is innovation a byproduct of structure, but so are sales, profitability and even company politics.

Consider that the nature of humans within organizations is fairly consistent and that, in general, professional people want to do their best. As a result, it is also natural for them to think that "our" Accounting department, or our Sales department or "our" Marketing department is the best in the business. It is the nature of high-performing professionals to be competitive and they all want to believe this. When we look at this objectively though, are the individual talents and skills really that much different from competitor to competitor? Are we just showing our own human tendencies and bias? It would be natural to do so.

To this point, I was involved in a major acquisition where we integrated "their" marketing, sales and accounting professionals with ours. I was genuinely surprised to learn how so many of their people were absolutely just as talented, hard working, and effective as our people! The rank and file people who run the business every day and who are in the trenches are pretty much the same in top-notch organizations. Are they essential? Absolutely. Are they valued? They had better be. However, among top-notch organizations, they are more similar than they are different.

It is proposed that the truly meaningful differences between leading organizations can be boiled down to two areas:

1) Leaders
2) Structure (with its associated processes and procedures).

This may be another way of saying that if the players are all about the same, then the team with the best coaches and the best playbook will win.

Outstanding leaders are always in short supply and the perfect structure will prove elusive. I suspect that very few CEOs think to themselves, "I have too many exceptional leaders, and I'm at a loss as to what to do with them all". In a similar way, it is suggested that there are very few CEOs who believe that their company is perfectly structured. If this was the case everything would be running smoothly, and this never reflects reality. Structure is something that is almost constantly being tinkered with to respond to the ever changing business environment.

It is when outstanding leadership and best-in-class structure are combined that you've hit a homerun. This situation also tends to attract and retain talent across the organization and as a result a positive productivity loop naturally entails. That's nirvana.

So how does this all apply to innovation? It begins by asking three fundamental questions.

1) How has your organization specifically structured itself to become more innovative?
2) How does your reward system stimulate innovation?
3) How do you measure the results associated with innovation?

The answer to the first question is either a) "we have an R&D department and we spend X millions on research" or b) "what do you mean?" or c) "we really don't". Of course the presence of an R&D department doesn't mean that an organization is particularly innovative, or even creative. After all, virtually all organizations have an R&D department.

I can speak from first hand experience about R&D departments and how their outputs are connected to leadership and structure. I've worked in R&D at three different companies in two very different industries. My first two jobs after graduate school were in R&D in the food industry. These two companies approached R&D quite differently. The first company I worked for was very academically oriented. The VP of Research was a retired PhD from a major university that specialized in food science. He was true to the scientific method and was well respected in the academic community. Our VP was well meaning but lacked leadership. He was often behind closed doors or in the company library. He was a bit of a recluse. This man was a research purist but had virtually no business acumen. He had fallen in love with science for its own sake. It seemed like the next step was always that more research had to be conducted. This approach was not very effective in driving business results as you can imagine. There was a big chasm between what Sales needed to sell and what R&D could commercialize in any reasonable period of time. The R&D culture was one of perpetual tinkering with no real pressure to deliver. Its people were frustrated too and a lot of them ended up leaving the company. Sales and Marketing people were looked upon as some sort of nuisance by the R&D staff. This culture felt a bit like a continuation of graduate school. To say the least, this wasn't very productive or rewarding.

The second company I worked for in a R&D capacity, the Ralston Purina Pet Care Company, had a dramatically different approach. This was a company that was new products driven. R&D worked directly with the Marketing department on a weekly basis. We knew what consumers wanted and we knew that the consumer was king. This thinking drove everything that was done. In this company there was a very real focus _applied_ research, not just fundamental research. Nobody cared if you had a PhD or not, they just wanted you to produce a new product that could be manufactured in the plants as soon as possible. They gave you the tools, a budget, a pilot plant, equipment, and technician support to do the job. The rest was up to you. The end result was clear. The means to that end was a rich ground for innovation.

Monthly status meetings were really "show-and-tell" sessions. In these we would physically share our latest products with our peers and management. It was a time to be proud and compare yourself to your contemporaries. It was stressful, yet competitive and good. There was accountability. They also encouraged you to look at new products and processes that went way beyond what was currently available. They encouraged you to dream and even had a name for it - "blue sky". They didn't mean BS either. They supported, and encouraged the notion of taking time every week to look up at the sky and think about what was next. They wanted to know what your ideas for the future were. You were *expected* to have ideas about the future. There was a balance between the here and now and the future.

I took these key experiences with me (plus Marketing and Sales experience) when management asked me to start up a new "solutions and capabilities team" to support our sales force of 500+ people. My approach was to keep all the good, but throw out the bad, from what I had learned. My charge was to create a team that would provide valuable tools and solutions that our sales guys could then leverage for competitive advantage. Our team's mission statement included language about "creating the future" and "rewriting the rules of the industry in our favor." Our team was designed from the beginning to commercialize innovation. Our goal was to deliver practical solutions that generated sales while simultaneously being a great team to work with.

Long story short, this team became tremendously successful. It literally earned every company award available and even inspired some new ones. More importantly it helped the sales team drive record growth *every* year for five consecutive years. Some of its solutions included:

- The Organization's Learning Centers (described in the beginning of the book), which 1) have been significant source of competitive advantage, 2) were featured in the company's annual report, and 3) have been referred to in the Wall Street Journal.
- Multiple new merchandising tools that generated over $30 million dollars in areas that were not previously considered.
- New tools and structures that allowed brands to come to life at retail like never before.
- Multiple best-in-industry practices.
- New technologies were created, proven and patented (both domestically and internationally).
- New solutions were developed that allowed the company to win in channels of distribution where they were previously ineffective.
- Joint ventures which delivered breakthrough solutions

- The development of new leaders

I think what was most rewarding of all is that we never got scooped. Our sales guys never came back to us and said, "here's what our competition is doing, why didn't you guys think of this first?" Our team lived by a slogan, "our competition will catch on, but they will never catch up". A certain fear of failure and personal pride in our work was very much a motivating force. I could go on forever about the specifics of what was learned through these experiences, but I feel what is most important are the general lessons that can be applied to any organization.

These will be applied within the context of the three questions posed earlier:

1. How is your company structured to deliver innovation?
2. How does your reward system stimulate innovation?
3. How do you measure your results?

Of course, all of these questions are interrelated and lead to the process for nurturing innovation.

The Process for Nurturing Innovation in Your Organization

If you truly want innovation then select the right people, make it their full-time job, hold them accountable, provide funding, give them a good leader who knows how to motivate, reward them, and then get out of their way. Give them a clear challenge not a tactical to-do list.

Let's examine each thought in more detail.

1. <u>Select the right people</u>. It is very important to select highly passionate people who exude the four pillars, have high energy and are eternally optimistic. It may not matter how educated or "smart" they are, because if they are not passionate and optimistic, or are low-

energy types, breakthrough innovation will not occur. When selecting the right people ask them a lot of questions. Here are some examples to consider:

- How would your friends and relatives describe you?
- Would your friends describe you as a passionate person?
- Can you share with me an example of when your passion allowed you to persevere through adversity?
- Can you share with me a time where you used humor to defuse a potentially contentious situation?
- What are the things in life that you are most passionate about?
- What are the things in your work and career that you are most passionate about?
- How would you ideally realign your work with your passion?
- Would your friends and relatives ever describe you as a risk-taker?
- What is the riskiest thing you have ever done that has led to a breakthrough in perspective, wisdom or results?
- What is your vision for a different future in your work, and in our industry?

Passion and optimism are the ingredients that will get them through when everyone else tells them they are nuts or wrong. Remember, passion is the catalyst that enables the other pillars of innovation. Don't hesitate to put your <u>very best people</u> in these positions.

2. <u>Structure for Innovation and make it someone's full time job</u>. To truly deliver innovation in your organization, then your structure must reflect that it is someone's fulltime responsibility. This is easy to see in the world of product R&D for example. You wouldn't think of it any other way. Where it gets less clear is in those departments that normally don't have an R&D component. How about in Sales, Manufacturing, Supply Chain, Information Systems or Accounting? If you really want breakthrough innovations in those disciplines as well (and not just incremental, zero-risk, low-leverage innovations), then it must be structured that way.

For example, do you want your <u>sales organization</u> to be more innovative? Then structure for it – make it someone's (or some team's) full time job. I've heard it said, "Everyone in sales is innovative, it's part of their job". Remember our definition of innovation though – that which is "new, new". Having been in sales, I can say with conviction that sales guys are highly resourceful and creative to the point of scheming, <u>but they are not</u> innovative. They will go with the tried and true until hell freezes over. They will push the same button that worked in the past until that button doesn't work anymore. This is exactly what they are paid to do. They are paid to execute, not innovate. Sales guys live from deal to deal and are rewarded to deliver the sales goal. For sales people, the future is now – right now. They have zero time and precious little incentive to think about the future (i.e. those breakthrough strategies that will allow them to win next year and beyond). It's not their fault, and it's not a criticism), it's just not their job or inclination. We often see some creativity in sales, but it's almost always in the guise of rehashed tactics that have worked in the past. Real breakthrough innovation in sales is rare (unless you structure for it).

To get really serious about delivering breakthrough innovation in *any* department or discipline, it ideally needs to be someone's full time responsibility. To act otherwise will jeopardize the organization's ability to innovate and successfully transition into the future. Failure to *structure* <u>for innovation in some way means that long term strategy is based on hope by default.</u> One definition of insanity is expecting different results without changing anything. Said another way, if you want different results, including breakthrough innovation, then things will have to be done differently.

Structure-related questions to ponder:

- Does your organization have a CIO - Chief *Innovation* Officer? If not, why not? Ten years ago companies didn't have Chief Information Officers either.
- Commercialized innovation is the key for a successful transition to the future. How is your current structure allowing that to happen?
- What messages are being sent to your organization about the importance of innovation by the way it's structured?

---

3. <u>Hold them Accountable.</u> People want to be held accountable. They want to know what the rules are and what the measurements will be. They want, and need, discipline. The key is focus. Teams that are responsible for delivering breakthrough innovation must craft a mission statement that spells out exactly, a) what their role is, b) how that role fits with the larger whole, and c) how they will be measured. The team's mission statement must make sense. It should capture the essence of their responsibility to the organization. There should be no room for ambiguity. This is important because a carefully constructed mission statement will help keep people on task and focused. The mission statement should be read at the beginning of every significant team meeting. Ambiguity is a stressor. Smart leaders eliminate the uncertainties. The mission statement should also spell out exactly how the team's work fits in with the larger objectives of the organization. In the case of the team I led which worked with the Sales Organization, we tapped directly into the Sales' force "value proposition" or strategy. This way we could be sure that we were on track and adding value. Our specific measures included:

- New sales tools which delivered __ $ this year.
- New solutions which facilitated __ new distribution in __ channel of trade.
- New processes which saved __ amount of money.

Take care to create a good mission statement up front. When team members know exactly what the rules are, and how they are going to be measured, it is liberating. They are set free to do their best work.

4. <u>Provide Funding</u>. Marketing, R&D and Sales departments cannot function without a budget. The same is true for innovation. Funding is needed. The <u>best way</u> to support your innovators is to give them a budget and give it to them upfront. This act is very motivating to innovators as is demonstrates trust. Don't make them jump through hoops every time they need some money. If you do, two bad things are certain to occur, 1) their projects will suffer serious delays and, 2) your innovators will be demoralized if they have to "beg for money from bureaucrats". Of course bureaucrats haven't a clue regarding the innovator's vision, and are motivated <u>not to innovate</u>. A bureaucrat's job is to perpetuate, not innovate.

The second best way to provide funding is to place the funds in the hands of a high-level executive who is a visionary. Do not put the money in the hands of your department heads. They will be too close to their own functional area to see the big picture and will be too tempted to hold the funds back to cover their own shortfalls.

The good news is that the money that is set aside does not have to be excessive. At a minimum, money must be available for beta testing. Generally these are very, very small amounts compared to the total size of the business.

5. <u>Choose the Right Leaders.</u> It is critical to pick the right leaders who 1) know how to think conceptually and, 2) know how to motivate and reward innovators. These are two separate skills. Picking the right leader isn't easy. Someone who is successful in one area of the business could be a total failure when it comes to leading the innovation process. The leader has to understand the long and short-term balance required. If the focus is all long-term, the urgency to deliver results will be completely lost. If all the focus is all short-term, you will never deliver the kind of breakthrough innovations that take time to nurture. It's always a balance. The leader who is too academic or long-term focused won't cut it nor will the manager whose only experiences have

been intensely short-term or tactical. If the right leader is chosen, the team will be able to deliver short-term innovations on a consistent basis, and larger breakthroughs which were the result of several years of incubation.

"Process, process everywhere, but not a vision in sight"
Robert Fritz – The Path of Least Resistance

Leaders responsible for delivering innovation must have vision and the ability to conceptualize. I have discovered that the ability to visualize varies greatly among individuals. It also appears to be independent of intelligence or title. You can be presenting a concept (e.g. an artist's rendering of a new design) to two equally successful, and intelligent, executives in the same room. The presenter states, "Now keep in mind this is a concept meant to convey the direction we are headed". Executive #1 will understand and his questions will reflect his ideas about <u>the concept</u>. Executive #2 will not get it. He will ask questions like, "why is that part blue?" or "shouldn't this piece be a litter bigger?" It is just not in his nature to understand that this is a concept. This type of person is a literal and tactical thinker. Regardless of how you try to engage this type of person, it is unlikely that you will get through. DO NOT put this personality type in charge of innovation efforts!

My experience also suggests that there is a direct link between one's ability to visualize and conceptualize and the degree to which that person has cross-functional experiences. For example, "Susan", who had experience in Accounting, R&D, and Sales generally, has a higher capacity to visualize ideas than does Bill, who has only been in Marketing. The bottom line is that some people will have virtually no ability to visualize something until it is fully developed and sitting right in front of them.

The last responsibility of the leader is to give the team the support and rewards that they need. Support comes in many ways. People whose responsibility it is to innovate need constant moral and emotional support. They need an ear to listen and a heart that cares. They particularly need this when the organization cannot see the innovator's vision or is indifferent. When their work doesn't ring a bell with everyone it is imperative though that it rings a bell with their leader. He or she must encourage them to keep going when others don't understand or appreciate the relevance of what they are doing and going through. Skeptics will abound and this can get people down. There will be people who mean well and will explain why certain ideas will never work. There will be people that have "data" to back up their point of view as to why things won't work. In extreme cases, there can even be slanderous comments directed towards the innovators as they are doing "different things" and therefore, "are not team players", "cannot be trusted", or "are not following the rules".

The leader, and top Management, must also understand what motivates innovators. Here's the long and short of it. It's not all about money. Nobody on our long list of world-famous passionate innovators was motivated by money, not Mother Theresa, not Louis Armstrong, not FDR, John F Kennedy, Jesus, or Tiger Woods. They were all motivated by their own passion to accomplish something great. That's what motivates innovators – the act itself – the act of creating the future (and fulfilling their own destinies if you will) because it can be done.

The research consistently shows that there is little or no correlation between monetary rewards offered and innovation delivered. The leader needs to understand this. He or she needs to show great interest in what the innovators are up to. The leader must be a good listener and encourager. The leader must show support via helping the innovators sell ideas internally, getting projects and budgets approved and getting recognition. The currency that most innovators are most interested in is in being appreciated for their work and accomplishing something that hadn't previously been done. It's not that money is irrelevant, but to an innovator, money is more likely to be perceived as a reflection of the degree to which she is appreciated.

Compare and contrast this to a sales role. These guys are almost always highly competitive and are most certainly motivated by money. Sell X and you can earn Y. That's the deal plain and simple. Sales people don't really have a passion for <u>what</u> they sell per se (e.g. diapers, dog food, plywood or motor oil) – who would? But they love the challenge of selling and the prospect of making money as a byproduct. It's critically important to understand the difference in what motivates people if you are a leader of innovation.

The last thing the leader should do is be patient and generally stay out of the way. Great innovators are almost exclusively self-starters. They don't need the stick. Ask a lot of questions and show genuine interest in their work but also give them enough "leash" to be comfortable. It shows that you trust them and trust is a powerful motivator!

The Buddy System

If there is an important opportunity that requires innovation, don't put one person on it, put two. There are many advantages to the "buddy system". First of all, by combining two really high-energy people, all kinds of synergy can occur. Innovators need other people to bounce their ideas off of. If they have a full-time buddy to do this with, the process can be greatly accelerated and the results will be better. The second reason this makes sense is because they need each other for moral support. Again, when other people just don't understand the vision of their work, or are indifferent or even slanderous, it is invaluable to have a buddy (and a boss that backs you up!).

An effective variation on the buddy system is the "Tom Sawyer system". From the Mark Twain classic <u>Huckleberry Finn</u>, you will recall how Tom got his friends to pay him for the privilege of whitewashing his fence. There are some wonderful dynamics at work here. People will provide their services for free if they are getting perceived value in return (e.g. the pleasure of painting the fence with a select group of peers). I have seen several examples of this in the area of innovation. Specifically, the innovator can draft whitewashers as needed from across the organization if the innovation project itself is perceived to be fun, career building, or both. If these conditions exist, other people in the company will volunteer some of their time to be part of the program.

There is a variation of the Tom Sawyer system that can be effective until a greater commitment to innovation is practical. In this variation, "Tom" is one of the top officers in the organization, and the whitewashers are all volunteers who are the passionate innovators.

Have them report directly to the President on a special project basis. Three excellent outcomes of this structuring are likely.

- The innovators will be highly motivated knowing that they have the explicit support of a top person.
- The whole organization will be sent a <u>powerful message</u> about how the top brass values innovation.
- The Top officers will have a stake in what is being developed and will feed off the enthusiasm of the innovators and provide invaluable wisdom along the way.

However you look at it, it's very difficult to deliver innovation in a vacuum. Make sure to consider the social aspects of your innovation structuring and encourage buddies.

Chapter 8 Key Learning

- Every organization is perfectly structured to get the results that it does.
- Nurturing innovation and structuring for innovation is different from other functional disciplines. Always remember to:
- ✓ Choose innovation team members and leaders *wisely* –those with vision, energy, and outstanding people skills
- ✓ Craft a quality mission statement
- ✓ Strike a balance between the long and the short term
- ✓ Make the innovators accountable through measurable results
- ✓ Be prepared to do some things differently

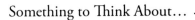

Something to Think About...

- How can you select for innovative people?
- How does your organization's structure foster or inhibit innovation?
- Is anyone working on innovation full time?
- How are people held accountable in your organization for results?

Chapter Nine –
Stop Thinking Outside The Box!

While the focus of the last chapter was on nurturing innovation within your own organization, the focus of this one will be on nurturing innovation through somebody else's. In other words, this involves hiring outside agencies to help you innovate. Examples of these agencies include advertising agencies, promotion agencies, public relations firms, design firms, consulting firms, etc. The important connection is that the innovation that you need is something that they have to deliver. This chapter focuses on the best ways of working with these people to deliver that product.

Thinking INSIDE the Box

The phrase "think outside the box" has become very popular. The implication of course is that thinking outside the box will lead to new thinking. New thinking can certainly be a good thing. However, when it comes to delivering innovation, we actually need to think <u>INSIDE THE BOX.</u> Here's why. Thinking outside the box implies a free-for-all of impulsive and creative thought. No borders and no boundaries. However, what the creative teams inside these agencies actually need is just the opposite! This may sound counter-intuitive, but it makes perfect sense.

To do their best work they have to know about all the parameters of the box. They need to know all the restrictions and realities, up front. They need to know the truth about your business, your competitors, your consumers, your profit objectives, etc. The worst mistake the hiring party, or client, can make is too give the agency too much freedom. Like most mistakes in life, the intentions are good. You'll hear comments like:

- They are so creative that I don't want to restrict them.
- You should see their work, if they could do something like that for us, it would be great.
- You are the agency, so we are really counting on you to tell us.

Some clients think that they are doing their agency a favor in communicating, "Go do your creative thing and get back to us". Nothing could be further from the truth. This is very unfair and frustrating to the agency. They absolutely need to know the parameters of the box. This makes perfect sense. You wouldn't say to your architect, "Just go do your architect thing!" If you were building a house with an architect you would want him to know, up front, the following:

- Your budget
- Your timeline for moving in
- Your location
- # Bedrooms and baths
- Square footage range
- Your lifestyle
- Preferences in materials

It is no different when working with an agency that is charged with developing an innovative solution for you. They need to know the parameters of the box. Get them inside the box. A box has four sides, a bottom and a lid. Explain what each of these parameters looks like in detail.

Imagine an in-store promotion agency is hired to kick-off the introduction of a new razor product for women. The following would need to be shared in detail.

- Budget restrictions – How much money is earmarked for this promotion, what <u>your</u> profit parameters are, and what the profit expectations of the <u>retailers</u> are.
- Timeline – When the promotion needs to be fully implemented in stores.
- Locations - Where these promotions need to be executed – what types of stores (e.g. grocery, Wal*Marts, Convenience stores, Department stores, etc).
- What the execution hurdles and realities are – The physical dimensions of the display pieces, the method in which it must be shipped, the degree to which in-store labor can be used to perform assembly, the pallet configuration (e.g. no more than four display pieces per pallet), etc.
- Who the consumer is that will be buying the product – This includes consumer demographics, consumer profiling research, how she needs to be communicated with <u>in the retail environment</u> and much more.
- What your expectations are and how they will be measured – e.g. "Our goal is for 50% of our target stores to have the display on the floor by the second week of March, driving purchases of 250,000 trial units and boosting market share 25% higher than in those retailers who didn't accept the display unit"

Execution of a concept can make or break everything. My experience has shown that it is wise to spend a lot of time here. Wherever there is the potential for a misstep, make sure that your agency is extremely well informed. There is always the potential for execution breakdowns in the retail environment. Make sure that you spend at least one full day with your agency at retail – two would be better. When you're in stores, always <u>talk to the people who work there</u>.

- Talk to the people in the backroom who receive and unload promotional displays. Ask them about the best promotion and worst promotion they have personally handled. You may learn that easy-to-follow picture instructions are greatly preferred or that bi-lingual instructions are important or that a significant number of employees can't read.

- Talk to people who stock shelves and sweep floors. You may learn, for example, that there is a law that requires the grocer to clean his floors every night. As a result, if the merchandising display piece isn't on wheels and mobile (i.e. and out of the way of the buffer machine), it will never be accepted by the buyer in first place.
- Talk to the store manager. He may tell you that his labor pool is very tight and that anything that requires assembly is not going to get out on his store floor (i.e. it will be headed to the dumpster!).

Bottom line: If you don't get dirty and do your homework, all your hard work and energy will end up in the dumpster.

The "Creative Brief"

The very first step in thinking inside the box is to develop a "creative brief". As the name implies, the brief is a one-page written summary of the challenge at hand. Writing the brief is also a lost art. Creative briefs should include the following seven steps and should always be shared face-to face with the agency.

1. The overarching objective – e.g. to support the introduction of a new product
2. The background – Why the product is being introduced, including the business dynamics, the competitive situation and the financial opportunity.
3. The budget and timeline – Money and time restrictions
4. Physical restrictions – Dimensions, technical constraints, etc.
5. Tone – The "feel" you are looking for
6. Execution considerations – Some things to consider in the execution itself and
7. The ideal verbatims – Beginning with the end in mind

The first four items have been reviewed in some detail. Items 5, 6, and 7 require additional explanation.

"Tone" refers to the feel of the work. Words that provide additional texture to the work will greatly aid the agency in their efforts to meet your needs. Using the example of the women's razor, words like feminine, soft, or tasteful would be helpful. Without them, the agency might think in terms of efficient, close shaving, or technically advanced. These are important distinctions. Tone can help focus the work.

"Execution considerations" refers to just that, things to consider in the final execution of the work. The key here is the positioning itself. These are considerations not dictates. Way too often, the client makes the mistake of jumping right to execution with his own ideas, even to the point of describing the end product. In one sense, that would be natural, you're just trying to help. In reality, you are not helping – you are in fact doing their job for them and not doing it very well. Don't dictate execution, if you already knew what to do, you shouldn't have hired the agency in the first place! Execution considerations allow you to share thoughts about how the final product could look without offending the people who are actually doing the work. In the example of the woman's razor, an execution consideration could be that, according to your research, women positively respond to photos of women shaving their legs. The research further showed that the women could then visualize how that razor would fit their hand and that this was important to them. This information would be very helpful to the agency. The consideration would be that somewhere in their execution they include a visual of a woman shaving.

The "ideal verbatim" will allow you and your agency to begin with the end in mind. The ideal verbatim should always articulate ideally what the target audience would say after seeing your product or innovation. Using the example again of the woman's razor, the ideal verbatim might go something like this:

Upon noticing the razor merchandising display in her local Safeway store, our target consumer would say, "hey, there is the razor that I saw on T.V. No more using my husband's razor, this one is made for me and my legs – I'm going to buy one right now"

To summarize, the creative brief serves to facilitate communication, and provides superior focus and grounding.

No substitute for TRUST

Make certain that your agency relationship is built on mutual respect. All human relationships are built on trust and respect. An agency relationship is no different. However, agency-client relationships can be particularly tricky! You can imagine what can happen when "business types" trying to sell more women's razors connect with "creative types" who love creativity for its own sake. In the worst case, the relationship can dissolve into animosity and name-calling. In the best case, innovative solutions are developed which take the business to a new level and a solid partnership is built.

Here are a few tips for maintaining good relationships.

- Communicate constantly – Face-to-face as the first option
- Have frequent updates to assess progress towards goals
- Clients: Acknowledge that <u>your agency</u> might have a terrific <u>business idea</u>.
- Agencies: Acknowledge that <u>your client</u> might have a terrific <u>creative idea</u>.
- Stay on time and on budget

When driving innovation through outside agencies remember to:

- Deliver a creative brief and discuss it with the agency face-to-face.
- Share all your consumer information, including any consumer research
- Do your homework together
- Introduce them to your business partners – both internally and externally
- Get them involved as equal partners in all your problems, opportunities and restrictions.
- Ask a ton of questions and make sure that they do the same
- Build a trusting relationship based on mutual respect.
- Get dirty and get out of the office. Remember, if you really want to know more about elephants, you have to talk to the keeper and grab a shovel.

In a nutshell, you will want to provide your agency with a well-defined box to think in. It is only through this process of laying out the restrictions that they can give you their best work. They will be more focused and energized and will thank you for it.

Chapter 9 Key Learning

- When working with outside agencies to deliver innovation, think inside the box.
- Communicate frequently – face to face and in writing.
- Focus on building a long-term, mutually beneficial partnership grounded in trust.

Chapter Ten – Summary

Throughout the ages it was believed that leaders were born, that the ability to lead was somehow inherited through the blood. Leadership, like height or eye color, was something that was simply bred. It was thought that the King was not only the rightful ruler but also the only one who was competent to lead (of course they had a vested interest in perpetuating this thinking and they used their power to do so!). In spite of many examples throughout history of blue-blood leadership ineptitude, birthright and competency became intertwined in the human psyche. This perception largely remained until the 20th century. Fortunately this myth did not stand up to the rigors of scientific scrutiny and the old thinking was replaced with the new. It was "discovered" that the ability to lead was not dependent on social class but rather that it was a skill that could be developed by anyone who was so inclined.

Similarly, the ability to innovate is <u>not</u> inherited. This is both good and bad news. The good news is that the ability to innovate is <u>a</u> skill and those who are willing can enhance their skills. The bad news is that by saying, "I'm just not an innovative person" you offer up an excuse, not a reason. That's like saying, "I'm just not the kind of person who speaks French". The truth is that French can be learned when you put enough effort into developing that skill. Millions of French toddlers do it every year. Of course, with any skill (e.g. musical, athletic, mechanical, etc), some people have greater aptitudes than others. The same is true with innovation and some do have a greater "innovation acumen" than others. At the same time, innovation can be honed and nurtured to the point where proficiency replaces inadequacy.

The bottom line is this, it's up to you and you can do it! This is a choice that you can make. You have already taken a good first step by reading this book. I hope that you have also begun to internalize the four pillars and have come to see them as self-evident. You can further hone your innovation skills by studying the Self-Help sections at the end of each pillar chapter. Feel free to tear these pages out and tape them to your mirror! This might be a good way of keeping the principles and exercises in front of you.

There's more good news, you don't have to be a genius to be an innovator. I'm living proof of that. I consider myself a common person who has had an uncommon journey. I am not a Steven Jobs or a Bill Gates or an Albert Einstein (and you probably aren't either), but we can be just as great, in our own right, by developing and leveraging our innovation skills.

The French mathematician and philosopher Rene Descartes is famous for the quote *"Cognito Ergo Sum"* or *"I think therefore I am"*. Descartes makes the direct connection between thinking and being alive.

The same is true about innovation, except maybe even more so. Consider this adaptation of that quote "I <u>innovate</u>, therefore I am".

If you are not innovating are you really thinking at your highest level?

And if you are not thinking at your highest level are you really living?

And if you are not innovating, thinking and living at your highest level, can you really enjoy success and happiness and all of life's abundance?

Innovation is directly linked to our own success and happiness and therefore innovation is very important. Innovation is not always urgent as you can put it off one more day like a diet, but it is undeniably and crucially important.

You can choose to be innovative by applying yourself and the four pillars. Consider this intriguing paradigm shift.

- Who are you NOT to be highly innovative?
- Who are you NOT to lead breakthrough innovation in your organization?

Reflect again on these great words and take them to heart.

Our worst fears are not that we are inadequate. Our worst fears are that we are powerful beyond measure. It is our light, not our darkness, that most frightens us.

We ask ourselves, "Who am I to be brilliant, gorgeous, talented, and fabulous?" Actually, who are you *not* to be? You are a child of God; your playing small doesn't serve the world. There is nothing enlightened about shrinking so that other people won't feel insecure around you.

We were born to make manifest the glory of God within us. It is not just in some of us, it is in everyone and as we let our light shine, we occasionally give other people permission to do the same.

As we are liberated from our own fear, our presence automatically liberates others.

Nelson Mandela, Inaugural Speech 1995

A final thought on Innovation

One day I heard a senior executive say, "I've been around here long enough that I don't believe in silver bullets".

Heaven help that guy. How sad. How common. What he is essentially saying is this, "I wouldn't recognize a breakthrough idea, or a paradigm shift in thinking, if it hit me right between the eyes". This guy is so set in his ways that he is blind even to the possibility of a different future. He would even be blind to a future where the rules of the game have been re-written in his own favor! Blind, that is, until you show him!

That is the role of the innovator. That is your supreme challenge and calling as an innovator – to envision that future, to create that future, to lead others and nurture that baby through to maturity. Nurture it to the point where everyone can "get it" and a culture of innovation becomes a reality.

We wish you all the best in this most worthwhile and relevant pursuit! Should you want any help along the way, let us know. This is our passion!

SOURCE NOTES

1. Deutsche Bank study, "Why TV Advertising Doesn't Work for Mature Brands", May 2004.
2. Senge, P. M. (1990). *The Fifth Discipline*. New York: Currency Doubleday.
3. Daft, R. (1998). *Organization Theory and Design, 6th ed.* Cincinnati, Ohio: South-Western College Publishing.
4. United States Navy Archives and Office of Naval Research.
5. Mass, P. (1999). *The Terrible Hours*. New York: Harper Collins Publishers.
6. Photos and diagrams courtesy of Milne Special Collections and Archives Department, University of New Hampshire Library, Durham, NH and the Office of Naval Research.
7. Joerding, J. A. (2000). The Impact of Individual vs. Group Training Using Expertise.
8. Joerding, J. A. (2002). A Model of Information Processing: An Analysis of the Influence of Expertise and Training on Group Performance, Group Efficacy, and Transactive Memory Systems.
9. "America's Richest Family". *Fortune.* November 22, 2004.
10. "America's Richest Family". *Fortune.* November 22, 2004.
11. Management Ventures, Inc. Boston, MA.
12. William Walsh, *The Rise and Decline of the Great Atlantic Tea Company.*
13. Management Ventures, Inc. Boston, MA.
14. Management Ventures, Inc. Boston, MA
15. Phil Lempert, *Being the Shopper,* 2002
16. AC Nielson Consumer Trends
17. Information Resources, Inc. Spring 2004.
18. Information Resources, Inc. Spring 2004.
19. Management Ventures, Inc. Boston, MA

Printed in the United States
73372LV00004B/36